THE FAITH AND FICTION OF MURIEL SPARK

The Faith and Fiction of Muriel Spark

Ruth Whittaker

First published 1982 by
THE MACMILLAN PRESS LTD
London and Basingstoke
Companies and representatives
throughout the world

ISBN 0 333 27297 8

Printed in Hong Kong

In memory
of my parents
Kenneth and Beryl Searle
with love

Contents

Acknowledgements

My thanks are due to all the people who have talked with me about Muriel Spark and her work. In particular, I am indebted to Professor Malcolm Bradbury, whose ideas I have found very stimulating, and with whom I have discussed much of the material in this book. I am extremely grateful also to Richard Webster for reading these chapters in draft form, and for his very helpful criticism of them. Finally, I should like to thank my husband, David Whittaker, for reading and correcting the final typescript, for his assistance with the index, and, above all, for his continual encouragement and support.

Westleton
Suffolk
1981   R.W.

1 The Sparkian Distinction

Muriel Spark's first published fiction was a short story called 'The Seraph and the Zambesi' (1951). Of this she said, 'I do not know what gave me the idea for the story, but certainly I believe in angels, and I had been up the Zambesi on a boat.'[1] Her assurance in acknowledging as inspiration both angels and boat-trips is characteristic, and her statement economically introduces the theme of all her work. This is the relationship – shown openly or implied – between the secular and the divine, between man's temporal viewpoint and God's eternal vision.

Such anachronistic interests on the part of a twentieth-century novelist have caused critics much unease in their attempts to categorise Mrs Spark. During the years of her development as a novelist, she has been identified with the Catholic Church, and also with such trends as 'social realism', the *nouveau roman* and 'post-modernism'. Thus, in the fifties and early sixties, when much of her work evoked a sense of place and history, she was considered primarily a realist for her precise observation and witty transcription of current mores and behaviour. Later, in the early seventies, her novels became novellas: short, sharp, highly structured, inviting comparison with the hard, impersonal quality of the *nouveau roman*. These novellas are reflexive, much concerned with the bare bones of structure, very little concerned with portraying the flesh of character or society. During this period Mrs Spark was regarded, indeed highly regarded, as an aesthetician, a writer with very formal interests insisting on the artifice of her medium. This critical pigeon-holing is complicated by the important fact that Mrs Spark is a Roman Catholic, but her novels are not deeply polemical, and her Catholicism never emerges as propaganda for the faith. Mrs Spark gives the impression of using rather than submitting to doctrines, of plundering for her own purposes. She satirises the extremes of social realism, exploits aspects of the *nouveau roman*, imbues her fiction with the irritable, reluctant quality of her personal faith. So, while her novels have an ethical and realistic bias, it is of a strange kind, refracted through techniques which serve to distance her realism. She has adopted twentieth-century technology, as it were, to deal with eternal truths; and, having suited her techniques to a sceptical and materialistic age, seeks to persuade us that angels and demons are neither metaphoric nor outdated conceits, but exist here and now in convents, classrooms and on the factory floor. In doing this she has remained peculiarly independent of pressures from both realism and the experimentalism of post-modernist fiction. But she has acknowledged them, felt them in her work, and it is worth looking briefly at these pressures in order to understand that the maintenance of a balance between them is a very considerable achievement.

Muriel Spark's first novel, *The Comforters*, appeared in 1957, and it contrasts strongly with the predominant tone of English fiction published in that decade. This tone has been well documented.[2] It was epitomised by writers such as Kingsley Amis and John Wain, who vigorously rejected any legacy of modernism, and by writers such as Alan Sillitoe and Stan Barstow, who wrote realistically and as if they never knew that such a legacy existed. This is not to say that no experimental novels were written in the 1950s; they were, and the definition of English post-war fiction simply as reaction against experiment has always been inadequate and misleading. Such a definition invariably omitted or distorted important writers such as Malcolm Lowry, Lawrence Durrell, William Golding, Anthony Burgess, Iris Murdoch and Muriel Spark, who were lumped together in a paragraph or a footnote as inconvenient exceptions to the rule. None the less, the most successful writers, in both critical and commercial terms, were those who articulated, realistically and comprehensibly, the frustrations and aspirations of many people at that time. These frustrations were largely social. The 1944 Education Act produced writers in the fifties who were the first generation in their families to experience both secondary and tertiary education. They then shared, broadly, the education of the middle and upper classes, but their background remained different, and this difference was frequently the subject of their new-found articulacy. The clash of values between what was known as the Establishment and the working class is a recurrent theme of fifties fiction, clearly illustrated in Alan Sillitoe's story 'The Loneliness of the Long Distance Runner'. Furthermore, the blurring through educational opportunity of formerly well defined social classes and the erosion of hierarchical authority (whether social, political or religious) led to a distinctive type of protagonist. This was the hero in search of his identity, an identity no longer defined clearly by his place in society and a code of unquestioned values. The attack on the established order, via their protagonists, led the writers of this period to be classed somewhat indiscriminately under the journalistic category of 'Angry Young Men', a label so pervasive that a 1957 review of *The Comforters* and other novels by women writers is headed 'No Angry Young Women?' In it the reviewer asks, 'Where are the angry young women, the female Jimmy Porters, the crazy mixed-up girls who should be brightening the literary scene?'[3] Clearly, Mrs Spark did not come into this category, and there are several reasons why.

The first is that, although she had been writing fiction for some years, Muriel Spark was thirty-nine when she published her first novel in 1957. This is considerably older than most writers of first novels in the 1950s, and her early work is without the theme of generalised youthful rebellion which typifies much of English fiction at this time. Secondly, Mrs Spark did not share the background of the majority of people who published their first novels in England in the fifties. She had attended a girls' school in Edinburgh, and then had lived abroad until she returned to Britain in 1944. She did not go to university, and it would be interesting to know how, and with what influences, she refined her scholastic gifts to those of the accomplished, mature poet who emerges in the late forties and early fifties.

Her conversion and the consequent religious matter of her early novels are further reasons for their distinctiveness. The realist novel of the fifties reflects a lack of religious commitment; there is no benign or vengeful God in the background. In Muriel Spark's novels, however, man's actions take place within a divine framework, and are portrayed in the context of his relationship, or lack of it, with God. This different perspective is especially clear in *The Ballad of Peckham Rye* (1960), where, in choosing to describe a working-class community, she ventures close to the subject-matter favoured by other writers at the time. But, if we compare this novel with, for example, *Saturday Night and Sunday Morning* or *A Kind of Loving*, it is immediately apparent how far her novel exceeds straightforward realism. Dougal Douglas is not angry about social injustice in Peckham, but he is appalled by the state of ignorance and immorality he finds there. The difference between poverty and Holy Poverty is a theme to which Mrs Spark returns in *The Girls of Slender Means* (1963) and in both these novels she shows that one does not necessarily entail the other. In *The Bachelors* (1960) she satirises the equation of virtue and a working-class background in the character of Ewart Thornton. Ewart is a schoolmaster who seeks to impress his hostess by telling her of 'the real miner's cottage of his birth in Carmarthenshire where his father still lived, and the real crofter's cottage in Perthshire where his grand-parents had lived till late' (p. 108).[4] He boasts to Isobel,

> 'I was given a pair of stout boots every year at Easter. Most of my clothes were home made. We had outdoor sanitation which we shared with two other families —'
>
> 'Were you ever in trouble with the police?' Isobel said, looking round in the hope that someone was listening.
>
> Ewart looked gravely at a vase of flowers, as if searching his memory, but obviously he had lost ground. At last he said, 'No, to be quite honest, no. But I recall being chased by a policeman. With some boys in some rough game. Yes, definitely chased down a back street.' (pp. 108–9)

Mrs Spark's novels are not much concerned with social mobility or status, nor in material conditions as their indicators. She is more interested in the spiritual status of her characters, and does not discriminate between rich and poor; both are weighed and found wanting.

For a Roman Catholic the phenomenal world is summed up by Cardinal Newman's motto *Ex umbris et imaginibus in veritatem* – 'From shadows and types to the truth'. This truth is not the apprehensible world, but the divine one, and this means that most Catholic writers avoid as irrelevant the painstaking realism exemplified by authors such as George Eliot and Mrs Gaskell, for whom its practice is rather like a statement of integrity – an open, sharing of experience from which examples are offered and conclusions drawn. For Catholic writers mimesis has a kind of triviality, almost an immorality, since the real concern is with the inimitable. They have an impatience with realism because they are anxious to convince the reader not of the recognisable, ordinary world, but rather to make us believe in and respond to the extraordinary. Graham Greene, reviewing *The Quest for Corvo* in

1934, writes about Rolfe's life, his intense struggle between God and the Devil, and then goes on to comment,

> It is odd to realize that all the time common-or-garden life is going on within hailing distance, publishers are making harsh bargains, readers are reporting adversely on his work, friends are forming hopeless plans of literary collaboration. . . . They have quite a different reality, much thinner reality, they are not concerned with eternal damnation.[5]

The Catholic novelist is always concerned with 'eternal damnation', and, when realism is practised, it is used as a foil against which the authorial revelation of the divine action will shine more brightly. This revelation obsesses Mrs Spark, and, whenever our attention is drawn to the trivial and commonplace in her novels, it is invariably to show us that they contain elements of something extraordinary, that is to say, they function in her work not to establish a familiar world, but as demonstrably part of a divine and unfamiliar pattern. In contrast, the emphasis of humanist novelists is on the relationship of the individual with the external world, rather than with God. This entails a different perspective, since, unlike the Catholic, they usually feel it necessary to present their case from scratch, to build up a coherent, autonomous world with which to convince their reader. The Catholic novelist, on the other hand, proceeds from a given set of precepts which are not usually spelled out in the novel itself. This difference stems directly from what seems to be a Catholic disdain for phenomena (except as symbolic of, or as a manifestation of God's design) and a Protestant respect for the substantial things of this world. Consequently in Mrs Spark's novels worldly events are made subordinate to the demands of the God-centred plot. Politics and economic conditions, instead of being part of the integral fabric of the novels, as they are in the work of Mrs Gaskell, for example, are brought in as and when they are needed. Thus Fascism in *The Prime of Miss Jean Brodie* (1961) is not introduced to add historical verisimilitude to a novel set in the thirties, but as a convenient snare to trap Miss Brodie for quite another sin. In *The Girls of Slender Means* the Second World War is used to provide a bomb which in turn provides the hero with the opportunity for a revelation of grace, and we are left in no doubt as to which event is considered the more important. *The Abbess of Crewe* (1974), although inspired by the Watergate scandal, transcends the realistic comparison and becomes a timeless parable about power and corruption.

During Mrs Spark's career as a novelist the realist English novel has been influenced by literary trends from France and America. Influenced, but not redefined. Indeed, it would seem that the abiding characteristic of English fiction is its capacity to assimilate and utilise new tendencies while tenaciously maintaining its essential, realist shape. One of the dominant features of post-modernism is its cultivation of neutrality: a refusal (in France, painstaking; in America, exuberant) to confer value or significance on what is described. In France, particularly in the early novels of Alain Robbe-Grillet, this took the form of concentration on the quiddity of things, leaving them apparently free from authorial distortion. Nathalie Sarraute distrusted what she saw as the falsification of psychological response by conventional language, and the *nouveau roman* is seen by its exponents not so much as anti-realist, but rather as an intense redefinition of realism. In America the experiments seemed less earnest, an open acceptance of the plurality of contemporary cultural influences incorporated into novels by authors revelling in their lack of discrimination. The works of writers such as Donald Barthelme and Richard Brautigan have an immediacy, an amazing display of near-innocence of the realist tradition which is by-passed rather than defied. American new fiction was characterised by a sense of play, of the-novel-as-game, expressed in some cases through reflexiveness, stressing the fictiveness of the text and the anti-mimetic intentions of the undertaking. But, although they evolved differently, what both the French *nouveau roman* and the American new fiction had in common was their motivation; a dissatisfaction with realism as an accurate or appropriate mode to depict contemporary reality, coupled, indeed, with a denial that such a depiction is necessarily the function of the novel anyway. This, of course, is nothing new. The history of the novel is the history of such dissatisfactions, and methods of coping with them were often vital and ingenious. But, because we live in a period which gives rise to such acute anxieties about the novel form, the reasons for them are of special interest, since we feel them to be, however obscurely, diagnostic of our times.

A factor in the rejection of realism is a sense that the bizarre nature of twentieth-century life is beyond the compass of realist conventions. The idea of an absurd world, rivalling and outstripping the wildest imaginings of the would-be fiction writer, has become an accepted excuse for a loss of confidence by contemporary novelists. It is debatable, however, that this century appears more bizarre or fragmented to its participants than any other. John Donne, writing in 1611

'Tis all in peeces, all cohaerence gone;
All just supply, and all Relation:
Prince, Subject, Father, Sonne, are things forgot[6]

is echoed, less elegantly, by Saul Bellow writing in 1963:

Public life, vivid and formless turbulence, news, slogans, mysterious crises, and unreal configurations dissolve coherence in all but the most resistant minds. . . . Rebels have no bourgeois certainties to return to when rebellions are done. The fixed points seem to be disappearing.[7]

A feeling of dislocation is not endemic to our age only, but it does seem to have been peculiarly disabling to realistic writers in recent years. This is partly because the novelist is challenged, as never before, by what might be called the lay fiction-makers of our time: the media men, the public-relations network, the press secretaries. In the proliferated information and dramatisation fed to us by the technological media we have an ordering of experience which rivals the fictional act. The cameraman and the editor replace the author when nightly episodes of war or murder trials are shown on television, and the immediacy of what is seen is often considered more authentic than the artist's subsequent fusion of experience and imagination. Consequently some writers have abandoned the attempt to compete with reality by offering simply to co-operate with it; the techniques of the new journalism merge with the new fiction as the author abdicates his responsibility of creating character, accepting the felicitous plots granted by the real world. In addition, we have preorganised structures of thought such as psychology and sociology, the language of which short-circuits detailed literary exposition. There are brief clinical labels available for the situations described in *King Lear*, *Anna Karenina*, *Sons and Lovers* which, in an age of haste, have come increasingly to replace literature as sufficient accounts of such experiences.

A further reason for the loss of authorial confidence is the questioning of hierarchies in all areas. Authority has been eroded, so that the claims of the omniscient, realist novelist to tell us what is so has been seriously challenged. Hence the attempts to create fictions without authorial domination, jettisoning the conventions of plot, character, point-of-view, third-person narration, and resorting even to typographical and technical devices, such as holes in pages and books in boxes – all efforts to evade the élitist connotations of the author's omniscient role. Other writers have emphasised the fictionalist element by working within fabulous and autonomous worlds which are deceptively free of the constraints, conventions and probabilities of realistic writing. Those who were unable to reject realism with such panache turned their unease into a credo of self-doubt, by querying within their novels the possibility of realism, or the rightness of it. This introspection, though not new in fiction, was one of the familiar features of post-modern sensibility, and frequently took the form of an assertion of vulnerability. The novelist, instead of practising his power over the real, made his querying of that power a sufficient task. Robbe-Grillet sums up this attitude: 'L'écrivain, par définition, ne sait où il va, et il écrit pour chercher, à comprendre pourquoi il écrit.'[8] Such routelessness has been exploited by literary critics, many of whom have added to the insecurity of the novelist by taking a lead and becoming authors in their own right. Authors, that is, not of novels, but of what Jonathan Raban has called 'criction':[9] critical fictions postulating theories about the nature of literature which are prescriptive rather than descriptive. 'Criction', in short, begins to precede fictions, and this can make the novelist's role uncomfortably parasitic. Such a situation is potentially dangerous to the health of the novel, overlapping as it does with Barthes's formulation of the critic's task as not 'to *discover* the work under consideration but, on the contrary, to *cover* it as completely as possible with one's own language'.[10] No wonder the novelists' authoritative stance has been eroded, and no wonder that they are acutely aware of it!

Mrs Spark's novels reflect, but never wholly assent to, the suppositions of the French new novel. In an interview in 1971 she named Robbe-Grillet as a modern novelist she admired, 'though I don't in the least accept the theory of the anti-novel'.[11] Her middle novellas, particularly, are influenced by the *nouveau roman* and she avails herself of a variety of its techniques. These include reflexiveness, use of the present tense, minutely detailed description given in a neutral tone, and narrative discontinuity involving the sacrifice of suspense. In addition, the subject-matter of her later novels is the absurdness and contingent quality of the modern world, and topics such as inflation and terrorism are presented as exempla of it. None of this, however, amounts to a rejection of omniscience, because Mrs

Spark believes in God, and for her the disparate elements of reality are bound together by her awareness of God's immanent, though often mysterious purpose. This purpose may be mirrored in the authority of the novelist. In *The Mandelbaum Gate* (1965), her most explicitly religious novel, she gives her protagonist's opinion of the *nouveau roman* as 'repetition, boredom, despair, going nowhere for nothing, all of which conditions are enclosed in a tight, unbreakable statement of the times at hand' (p. 188). Such a view, suggesting the solipsistic, nihilistic nature of the *nouveau roman*, makes it an inadequate medium for Mrs Spark, since for her the 'times at hand' are not properly or fully explained by reference only to 'repetition, boredom, despair'. These conditions, she suggests, both sustain and reflect the *nouveau roman*, which perpetuates through its style the world it describes. For Muriel Spark, however, there is 'another world than this' (*The Ballad of Peckham Rye*, p. 202), a world which encompasses possibilities of faith and redemption, factors qualifying and lessening the 'boredom and despair', and, in her novels, ultimately transcending them. Therefore, although there is a similarity between some of her writing and that of the new French novelists, her use of their techniques is not mimetic (that is to say, as appropriate for 'the times at hand') but didactic. She uses them, not as a sufficient account of the world, but to illustrate the inadequacy and danger of erecting a stylistic corral which by its very nature excludes entry to elements which might negate its existence. Thus, when she describes things in clinical, neutral detail, it is a method of alerting us to the mood of a situation, or to the neurosis of a character. In other words, she subverts the original function of techniques designed in part to convey stasis and quiddity, by using them dynamically, towards an end. The highly specific nature of a novel such as *The Driver's Seat* (1970) becomes a joke of some importance at the expense of the *nouveau roman*, since we are shown that whatever appears contingent or simply *there* in all its specificity is, nevertheless, finally subject to the demands of an old-fashioned, significant plot.

Mrs Spark's designs are illustrated in a passage from *The Driver's Seat*, where the protagonist's apartment is described with deceptive neutrality:

She has added very little to the room; very little is needed, for the furniture is all fixed, adaptable to various uses, and stackable. Stacked into a panel are six folding chairs, should the tenant decide to entertain six for dinner. The writing desk extends to a dining table, and when the desk is not in use it, too, disappears into the pinewood wall, its bracket-lamp hingeing outward and upward to form a wall-lamp. The bed is by day a narrow seat with overhanging bookcases; by night it swivels out to accommodate the sleeper. Lise has put down a patterned rug from Greece. She has fitted a hopsack covering on the seat of the divan. Unlike the other tenants she has not put unnecessary curtains in the window; her flat is not closely overlooked and in summer she keeps the venetian blinds down over the windows and slightly opened to let in the light. A small pantry-kitchen adjoins this room. Here, too, everything is contrived to fold away into the dignity of unvarnished pinewood. And in the bathroom as well, nothing need be seen, nothing need be left lying about. The bed-supports, the door, the window frame, the hanging cupboard, the storage space, the shelves, the desk that extends, the tables that stack – they are made of such pinewood as one may never see again in a modest bachelor apartment. Lise keeps her flat as clean-lined and clear to return to after her work as if it were uninhabited. The swaying tall pines among the litter of cones on the forest floor have been subdued into silence and into obedient bulks.   (pp. 19–20)

Far from being neutral, however, this precise description implies a range of meaning. Mrs Spark uses even the simplest language as metaphor, so that its very bland quality sends alarm bells ringing in our minds. In this passage there is a sense of inflexibility, of over-tidiness, of pointless ingenuity. The flat is highly self-contained, and this extends by association to Lise, reflecting her fatal self-sufficiency: she would never borrow a cup of sugar from a neighbour. She keeps herself to herself, her blinds down, her existence 'clean-lined and clear . . . as if it were uninhabited'. The messy evidence of humanity does not show itself either in the flat or in her life, and in the final sentence of this passage Mrs Spark confirms this tragedy, which is implicit in the description preceding it. She does this by using an open metaphor, thus guilty, in Robbe-Grillet's terms, of establishing a relationship between the world and the individual. The sudden lyricism of 'the tall swaying pines' and the weighted sadness of the verb 'subdued' contrast the trees with what they were and what they have become, dull 'obedient bulks'. This makes ironic, or at least qualifies, the earlier phrase 'the dignity of unvarnished pinewood'; dignity becomes, in retrospect, the veneer of submission. From a world defined by order within four walls we are shown a glimpse of something other, the beautiful but defeated possibilities of grace and freedom.

Similarly, Mrs Spark's use of reflexiveness has a purpose different from many contemporary writers'. Her assertions of fictionality are not made to proclaim the inadequacy of the realistic novel to reflect an absurd world, nor to turn the novel into a handbook of fictional theory. At the beginning of her career as a novelist the reflexiveness of *The Comforters* was a means of testing a new form. The traditional looseness of the novel was at first suspect to the former poet:

> I had resisted the novel because I thought it was a lazy way of writing poetry. . . . I had to sit down and write a novel about somebody writing a novel to see if it was aesthetically valid and if I could do it and live with myself, writing such a – as I thought – low thing as a novel.[12]

In addition, the reflexive nature of *The Comforters*, *Loitering with Intent* (1981) and Mrs Spark's novellas is used to disengage the reader from the wrong sort of involvement with the texts. When the narrator points out, in her first novel, that 'the characters in this novel are all fictitious' (p. 74) the reader is jolted from his 'suspension of disbelief' and forced to reconsider the novel as symbolic rather than as wholly realistic. He is reminded, in other words, that for Mrs Spark reality lies not in the novel nor in the everyday world, but in the realm of God. By sabotaging her own creation of an autonomous, fictional world she endorses her view of God as omniscient author. Thus she makes clear that what she writes is within his overall design, and even while the reader employs this world as a frame of reference it is shown to be an insufficient source of verification. In Mrs Spark's novels the reader has to engage with 'another world than this' for an understanding of her work.

I have tried to show briefly in the preceding pages that Muriel Spark is not a novelist committed to the English realist tradition, nor is she a writer concerned only with the revelation of the novel's structure. Her Christianity overpowers both endeavours, since her evocation of reality includes a transcendent world, and her novels, however much to do with fictionality, are written from a moral standpoint. She is perhaps more obviously resistant to the process of critical labelling than many writers because her direction and emphases change considerably in the course of her work; a tendency in one novel may be modified, intensified or nearly contradicted in another. At the beginning of her canon her novels were basically realistic, but shot through with reminders of the supernatural world, which appear peripheral but turn out to be central to the plots. Her five middle novellas – from *The Public Image* (1968) to *The Abbess of Crewe* (1974) – are to do with the exposure of fictions: those perpetrated by the media, or those created by the novelist. *The Takeover* (1976) and *Territorial Rights* (1979) are looser, the emphasis having shifted from a revelation of fictional techniques to a broad, ironic observation of the practice of deception in everyday life. *Loitering with Intent* reverts to an examination of the creative process. Nevertheless, her work does have consistent factors. The explicit or implicit expression of faith in a divine order is one; the other, and allied characteristic is the extreme detachment of her fiction. Throughout her work there is a sense of suppression, an air of controlled panic restrained through the use of rigorous, economic prose. It is as if the precision of the language might have an exorcising function, like stepping carefully over the cracks in the pavement. I want to examine this tension, since for me it seems highly significant and intrinsic to her work.

The most striking omission in Mrs Spark's work (with the exception of *Loitering with Intent*) is that of emotional expression; it is as though she cannot accommodate within her ordered prose the imprecision of passion. Anger is suppressed, refined into hatred, which breaks out in sudden and unexpected violence. People seldom have blazing rows in Mrs Spark's novels: they quietly kill one another instead. Sudden deaths occur frequently, but are always related with conspicuous coolness. For example,

He looked as if he would murder me and he did.
('The Portobello Road', *Collected Stories I*, p. 29)

He wrenched the stick from the old woman's hand and, with the blunt end of it, battered her to death. It was her eighty-first year.
(*Memento Mori*, p. 200)

He came towards her with the corkscrew and stabbed it into her long neck nine times, and killed her. Then he took his hat and went home to his wife.
(*The Ballad of Peckham Rye*, p. 193)

A V-2 bomb hits them direct just as the train starts pulling out. The back section of the train, where they are sitting, and all its occupants, are completely demolished.

(The Hothouse by the East River, p. 150)

Denied the expressions of shock, despair or authorial moralising that usually attend death in novels, the reader is forced to think instead of feel, to exercise a personal moral intelligence in each case, without explicit guidance from the author. This may be a useful discipline, but I am left, none the less, with a feeling of unease, which is intensified rather than alleviated by seeing how Mrs Spark deals with potentially loving relationships in her work. In fact, very few people love each other in her novels. Close relationships are more often based on a reluctant mutual dependence brought about by unsought proximity. When she does introduce lovers into a novel she describes them with an edge of irony or farce. Jean Brodie's lovers, past and present, are merely extensions of her ego. In *The Mandelbaum Gate* the principal love-affair is conducted with laconic self-mockery by its participants, the excuse being that they are 'academic intellectuals' (p. 42). In *The Girls of Slender Means* Nicholas is made capable of realising the discrepancy between Selina and his image of her, even while he succumbs to his idealised version.

Mrs Spark's lack of sentimentality can, however, be refreshing. In *Memento Mori* two old ladies attend a Mass for the soul of another who has died in hospital:

At eleven o'clock next morning Miss Valvona and Miss Taylor were wheeled into the hospital chapel. They were accompanied by three other grannies, not Catholics, from the Maud Long Ward who had been attached to Granny Barnacle in various ways, including those of love, scorn, resentment, and pity. (pp. 129–30)

The feelings of the other patients towards the dead woman are not given as uncritically affectionate, and in that way Mrs Spark makes their final tribute more significant. At the end of *The Mandelbaum Gate* we are told that 'Barbara and Harry were married and got along fairly well together ever after' (p. 329) and we appreciate the realism implicit in the parody of conventional happy endings. The novel is flawed, however, by the lack of convincing realism in their love-affair, which is central to the plot, and which needs our conviction.

Mrs Spark, while needing to convey the force of emotions, can often only write *about* them.

Many critics have commented on this inability without invariably condemning it. Reviewing *The Mandelbaum Gate* Warner Berthoff writes

> One feels that there is simply no place for the action of love in the world of free travelling English men and women that Muriel Spark clings to as a novelist, for all her sharpness about it. Or is it that love is the great occasion that her books reach out towards but that she cannot bring herself to write about directly, circumstantially?[13]

Douglas Reed puts it more forcibly:

> Miss Spark [*sic*] is taut, inhibited from fully tapping the primitive and romantic passions within herself, perhaps because they are too clearly related to the unknown terror ricochetting through her tales . . . not susceptible to calm reason. . . .[14]

Writing in the *New Yorker* John Updike appears ambivalent towards Mrs Spark's aloofness:

> Mrs Spark's simplicity is diagrammatic rather than sensual; her hard, unflecked prose seems laid on from a calculated distance that this admirer, sometimes, would be relieved to see reduced.
> But detachment is the genius of her fiction. We are lifted above her characters, and though they are reduced in size and cryptically foreshortened, they are all seen at once, and their busy interactions are as plain and pleasing as a solved puzzle.[15]

Frank Kermode, interestingly, sees a virtue in Mrs Spark's apparent callousness:

> There is certainly a remoteness, a lack of ordinary compassion, in her dealings with characters, but this is part of the premise of her fiction; if we feel sorry in the wrong way, it's because our emotions are as messy and imprecise as life, part of the muddle she is sorting out.[16]

Kermode, in this and subsequent reviews, commends Mrs Spark's ability to sort out the 'muddle' of our emotions through the pattern of aesthetic ordering, taking for granted that this is a commendable undertaking. He makes much of Mrs Spark's predilection for end-directed, uncontingent plots and her fusion of the eschatological interests of the Roman Catholic Church with the aesthetic teleology of the novel form. He claims her for a formalist as ardently as others have claimed her for a Catholic apologist, and such a definition is short-sighted. While it might be consoling in the short term for a novelist's inability to explore the world of emotions to be redefined as a literary aesthetic, it is not helpful in the long run because it tidies up the problem and makes it respectable instead of admitting that it is a problem. In *The Sense of an Ending* Kermode says, 'her reality is not the brutal chaos of which Ortega speaks, but a radically non-contingent reality to be dealt with in purely novelistic terms'.[17] Mrs Spark's best work, however, reveals that she is aware of the possible sterility in conveying her orderly, religious apprehension of the world solely in terms fitting to the non-contingency of her novels. Indeed, in *The Driver's Seat*, by creating a protagonist who is impelled by the necessities of plot-making and shown to be unable to accept the potential offered by emotional distractions, Mrs Spark brilliantly utilises her own limitations as a novelist. The result is a work of art precisely because of the evocation of emotional loss and not in spite of it.

When questioned by interviewers about the quality of detachment in her work, Mrs Spark is given to answering obliquely: 'I think it's bad manners to inflict a lot of emotional involvement on the reader — much nicer to make them laugh and keep it short.'[18] That sounds like a tip for an after-dinner speaker rather than a novelist's credo, but later it is expanded into the basis of a crusade. In an address to the American Academy of Arts and Letters in 1971, Mrs Spark condemns literature which arouses sympathy because it enables us to substitute feeling for action:

the art and literature of sentiment and emotion, however beautiful in itself, however striking in its depiction of actuality, has to go. It cheats us into a sense of involvement with life and society, but in reality it is a segregated activity. In its place I advocate the arts of satire and of ridicule. And I see no other living art form for the future.[19]

She goes on to suggest for all forms of art 'a more deliberate cunning, a more derisive undermining of what is wrong. I would like to see less emotion and more intelligence in these efforts to impress our minds and hearts.'[20] In *Loitering with Intent* there is a softening of this attitude, but certainly 'less emotion and more intelligence' (with the dangerous implication that the two are incompatible) was increasingly the formula for her novels up to 1981. Her justification of it, however, may be less altruistic than she makes out. It is a rationalisation of a mode she has always preferred, and its current relevance both to the world's absurdities and literary methods of dealing with them is a fortuity that she has skilfully utilised.

Muriel Spark's determined avoidance of emotional expression greatly affects her style, which is characterised by what could be called techniques of evasion. These include irony and satire, methods of detachment by the author which should, paradoxically, evoke in the reader a sense of involvement with the positive values negatively defined. Henry James, writing about irony, says, 'the strength of applied irony [is] surely in the sincerities, the lucidities, the utilities that stand behind it. . . . It implies and projects the possible other case, the case rich and edifying where the actuality is pretentious and vain.'[21] In her early novels, and in *Loitering with Intent*, Mrs Spark achieves this projection. She is able, totally without sentimentality, to draw attention to the need for faith and love. Often this is done obliquely by describing the consequences of their absence, by conjuring up a sense of loss so vividly that the omission of these qualities becomes a deliberate and eloquent reminder of their necessity. But in her five novels from *Not to Disturb* (1971) up to and including *Territorial Rights* (1979), these omissions do not give the same sense of a satiric or didactic withdrawal, designed to arouse concern; they are more nearly just omissions. Attention is drawn less and less to the absence of love and human pity, although satire and comedy abound, usefully distracting our attention and making us laugh. But the reader eventually senses that the distractions are merely entertainment, and that the ironic or satiric stance is in danger of becoming frozen. It is no longer the rhetoric of concern, but of detachment, and is used as protection against the threat of emotional vitality rather than as a lament for its absence.

Nevertheless, although I am made uneasy by Mrs Spark's evasive techniques in her later work, there is no doubt that her evasions are infinitely more elegant and occasionally more enlightening than some novelists' attempts to engage with emotional issues head on: attempts she parodies in *Territorial Rights*. Mrs Spark exploits her limitations, making them a source both of regret and of inspiration. This tension pervades her novels, and she skilfully uses it by making her protagonists subject to a similar dilemma. Their struggles are between the messy attractions of a full emotional life and the clean formality of plot, which is either the spiritual demands of God's plot, or the aesthetic demands of fiction-making. Muriel Spark's methods of delineation are complex, and in this chapter I have tried to disentangle some of them, to show that, while partaking of realist, experimental and Catholic influences, she remains peculiarly independent of any exclusive category. Realism is inadequate, since her concept of reality includes the divine and the supernatural. She uses experimental techniques, but negates their original functions by subordinating them to her own, religious vision of coherence. Her Catholicism, as expressed in her novels, is uncomfortable and idiosyncratic, and is far from a call to conversion. My definition of 'Sparkian', finally, includes the tension I detect in her work between feeling and form. In subsequent chapters I want to pursue this theme and its manifestations.

2 Background

Mrs Spark is intensely reticent, outside her novels, about her life. She rarely gives interviews, and, living in Italy, she keeps her distance from day-to-day literary gossip in London and New York. Her desire to keep private the story of her life seems related to her thrift as a writer. She gives the impression of being anxious not to dissipate her material; of hoarding it, with a novelist's awareness of its potential, and ultimately refining it through the alchemic process of her art. Indeed, the best account of Muriel Spark as an artist is given in her novel *Loitering with Intent*. This is clearly autobiographical, and extremely valuable in its revelation of how a writer's life and work are deeply interwoven. Nevertheless, to attempt to separate the strands is a relevant activity on the part of the literary critic, a point which Mrs Spark herself appreciated in her critical works on Mary Wollstonecraft Shelley, Emily Brontë and John Masefield. In these studies she includes their life-stories, from which she deduces a variety of influences on their writings. She has, however, warned of the dangers inherent in compiling biography from fiction: 'I believe that fiction should generally be considered a suspect witness (and if it is not stranger than truth, it ought to be).'[1] Naturally, biographical inferences from a novelist's work should be made with caution, just as interviews, correspondence, biography and autobiography should be regarded as approximations, facets of the truth, and not the whole story. But it is still possible to trace threads extending, as it were, between the real and the fictional worlds. In considering the evidence of Mrs Spark's novels in relationship to the available information about her life, I have tried to trace these threads, for it is clear that her upbringing and education, her conversion, her living abroad have all contributed substantially to her work.

Muriel Sarah Camberg was born in Edinburgh in 1918. Her father was Jewish, and she has said of her childhood that it had 'a kind of Jewish tinge but without any formal instruction'.[2] And when she was asked in an interview 'How important has it been that you're half-Jewish?' she replied, 'I don't particularly associate myself with Jewish causes. But I defend them sharply if they're attacked.'[3] In one of her short stories, however, 'The Gentile Jewess', and in the novel *The Mandelbaum Gate* she reveals that her mixed parentage has had a deep influence on her thinking, making her aware of the disparate elements in her make-up, and of the need to reconcile and come to terms with them. Mrs Spark apparently sees no religious contradiction between being simultaneously Jewish and Roman Catholic. In an interview with Malcolm Muggeridge she made the rather unorthodox observation, 'to my mind . . . the Catholic church is a continuation of the Jewish church'.[4] The Jewishness of Christ would seem a factor contributing to her view of the unity between the two religions, combining elements of both economy and divine irony which she enjoys so much, and which are significant motivations of her work.

Her literary ability was apparent at a very early age:

I remember that I could write — also it came down as a family legend that I could write before I could talk . . . I could put words together long before I went to school, and long before I really started opening my mouth to say anything, so that it was a natural gift.[5]

She went to James Gillespie's Girls' School in Edinburgh, which had a Presbyterian atmosphere and where, she says, she was 'the school's Poet and Dreamer'.[6] In a letter[7] written from Edinburgh in 1952 while she was visiting her mother, she mentions that she has discovered her earliest notebooks of poetry, and found that she used a wider metrical range at eleven than she had done ever since. Her writing was not confined to poetry. In an interview with Alex Hamilton[8] we learn that she kept a diary, and was also in the habit of inventing letters to herself from boyfriends, hiding them where her mother would find them. This strange activity seems like a bid for an emotional life of her own, constrained at the same time by a need to submit that life to control. It is indicative of her future craft as a novelist, the action of a plotter and a fiction-maker, creating situations analogous to those with real potential, but over which control can be exercised. Muriel Camberg's schooldays are captured in *The Prime of Miss Jean Brodie* and the atmosphere evoked is utterly convincing. The character of Jean Brodie is based on one of her teachers – not as she in fact was, but on her latent potential. Explaining this Muriel Spark has said,

> I think that children, and artists, have the capacity for discerning not only the characteristics of people but their potentialities. . . . there . . . were teachers at my school who had these potentialities themselves; perhaps they didn't know it themselves, but they must have betrayed it – and completely unrealised potentialities, because that's what Jean Brodie represents.[9]

The perceptive scrutiny of the schoolgirl was obviously formidable even then, since it emerges so powerfully in the novel over twenty-five years later.

Mrs Spark went straight from school to Rhodesia, where she married and had a son, Robin. The sudden transition from a schoolgirl in Edinburgh to a married woman in colonial Africa must have been dramatic, to say the least. Although Mrs Spark has never written a novel about this period of her life, some of her best and most evocative short stories are set in Africa, and the experience clearly made a profound and indelible impression on her. These stories are notable for the relative closeness of the author and the narratorial voice. Four of the six stories are narrated in the first person, and two – 'The Go-Away Bird' and 'Bang-bang You're Dead' – in the third person, largely from the viewpoint of heroines difficult to dissociate from Mrs Spark. Her expatriate eye sees the country itself as potentially savage and inhospitable:

> This was a territory where you could not bathe in the gentlest stream but a germ from the water entered your kidneys and blighted your body for life; where you could not go for a walk before six in the evening without returning crazed by the sun. . . it was a place where the tall grass was dangerous from snakes and the floors dangerous from scorpions.
>
> ('The Curtain Blown by the Breeze', *Collected Stories I*, pp. 35–6)

The urbane appearance of the European settlers seems to contrast with their uncivilised surroundings, but is shown to be a veneer only:

> At that time many of the men looked like Rupert Brooke, whose

portrait still hung in everyone's imagination. It was that clear-cut, 'typically English' face which is seldom seen on the actual soil of England, but proliferates in the African Colonies.

'I must say,' said Sybil's hostess, 'the men look charming.'

These men were all charming, Sybil had decided at the time, until you got to know them.

('Bang-bang You're Dead', *Collected Stories I*, p. 77)

These stories have something in common with Doris Lessing's early work; not just the location, but the sense of alienation from the white community and a rejection of its prevalent values. Muriel Spark's protagonists, like Doris Lessing's, attempt to create their own defences against the sterility surrounding them, which Mrs Spark often symbolises by an image of dryness, such as a desert or a dry river-bed:

Sybil lay in bed in the mornings reading the translation of Kierkegaard's *Journals*, newly arrived from England in their first, revelatory month of publication. She felt like a desert which had not realised its own aridity till the rain began to fall upon it. When Donald came home in the late afternoons she had less and less to say to him. (Ibid., p. 87)

Mrs Spark dwells on the isolation and claustrophobic atmosphere of the white expatriate communities, in which emotions are intensified. 'This place brings out *the savage in ourselves*', stresses a character in 'The Go-Away Bird', and the climax of almost all these stories is sudden violence, born of hatred and jealousy. Indeed, the narrative concern with adultery, jealousy, revenge and murder foreshadows the dramas in *The Takeover* and *Territorial Rights*, but the tone of the 'Africa' stories is entirely different. In her later novels Mrs Spark capitalises on the Italian predilection for strong emotions and high drama, and, as an outside observer, combines these elements with farce and exuberance in her fictions. Writing from her own close involvement and experience of Africa she conveys boredom and disgust at the life-style of her compatriots, and there is conjured up in these stories a sense of desolation unequalled in her novels.

In both 'Bang-bang You're Dead' and 'The Go-Away Bird' the heroines long to go to England, but are not allowed to leave the African continent because the Second World War has broken out. One may surmise that, like them, Muriel Spark was 'trapped' in

Africa against her will. Finally, in 1944, her marriage having broken up, she managed to return to England. For the remainder of the war she worked in a branch of the Intelligence Service based at Woburn Abbey. She was employed in a department run by Sefton Delmer, who was responsible for the output of anti-Nazi propaganda. This was evidently a useful grounding for Mrs Spark's interest in the process of creating fictions. She makes use of this experience in *The Hothouse by the East River* (1973), describing the work as 'black propaganda and psychological warfare ... a tangled mixture of damaging lies, flattering and plausible truths' (p. 61).

The years between the ending of the war and the publication of her first novel in 1957 were difficult for Mrs Spark. Financially, it was the toughest period of her life, and the struggle finally made her ill. These were years of apprenticeship, when she turned her hand to a wide range of writing, including work for a jewellery trade magazine, and as a press officer. Her main concern, however, was poetry. She had continued writing poetry after she left school, and in 1946 she had two poems published in the *Poetry Review New Verse Supplement*. In 1947 she became Secretary of the Poetry Society, and from 1948 to 1949 was Editor of the Society's magazine, *Poetry Review*. Her editorials were lively, and she was instrumental in encouraging younger poets to submit their work to the magazine, not least by taking the unprecedented step of paying them for poems published. The consequent impoverishment of the Society led, with other factors, to her dismissal in one of the Poetry Society's periodic upheavals. While at the Poetry Society Mrs Spark lived at the Helena Club in Lancaster Gate; her experience of this hostel, together with her increasing knowledge of the London literary scene, are drawn on in her early novels and in *Loitering with Intent*. After leaving the Poetry Society she began her own short-lived magazine, *Forum*, which was first published in the summer of 1949, but which ceased publication after two issues. Its contributors included Dannie Abse, Denys Val Baker, Robert Greacen, Herbert Palmer, Derek Stanford, Henry Treece and John Waller. The second issue was edited jointly with Derek Stanford, a poet and critic, with whom Muriel Spark collaborated on subsequent literary ventures.

In his book of reminiscences *Inside the Forties*, Stanford describes Muriel Spark's attractiveness and her appeal to men. In an interview in 1973 when asked if she had ever thought of marrying again, she replied, 'Oh yes ... Lots of times. But I would never make a good wife. You have to work at it, at things like being a hostess, and I've so much else to do.'[10] In April 1949, in a letter[11] describing the break-up of a relationship, she writes candidly that her fault was selfishness. She goes on to say that the man in question needed a woman who would have dedicated her life to him, something she was not prepared to do because she had to earn a living for her son, and when she was not doing that she wanted to write. In *Loitering with Intent* the heroine is asked if she is going to marry. 'No, I write poetry. I want to write. Marriage would interfere' (p. 27), she replies, shocking her questioner. In *Inside the Forties* there is an interesting photograph of Mrs Spark. She is elegantly dressed, and her appearance is feminine and delicate. But her eyes are wary, and her jawline and mouth signify the most extraordinary determination. Looking at the picture with hindsight, one has no doubt at all that its subject would succeed at whatever she determined on. Later photographs are more highly posed. This early photograph shows with great clarity both her sensitivity and her single-mindedness.

After leaving the Poetry Society Muriel Spark worked briefly for a publicity agent to earn money. She continued her own writing, however, and began collaboration on a number of critical works. These were mostly on nineteenth-century writers, linked only by the fact that the centenary of their deaths provided an occasion to interest publishers in them. The first book undertaken was an edition of Anne Brontë's collected works, with biographical and critical introductions by Muriel Spark and Derek Stanford respectively, but the publishers went into liquidation before the book appeared. In 1950 *Tribute to Wordsworth* was published, subtitled 'A miscellany of opinion for the centenary of the Poet's death'. 1951, the centenary of Mary Wollstonecraft Shelley's death, saw the publication of *Child of Light*. This was by Muriel Spark, and is a reassessment of Mary Shelley's life and work. It is a particularly interesting book since there are analogies between the lives of the two women. Both Mary Shelley and Muriel Spark returned to England after their youthful marriages had ended to begin new lives, each with a young son to support. Both women were hard up, and both earned money by writing. During their lives they outgrew their former friends, and later, when Mary Shelley's fortunes improved, she was subjected to blackmail, a theme to which Mrs Spark reverts frequently in her novels, and which clearly fascinated her as a facet of Mary's life. More importantly, we can find in Mrs Spark's understanding of Mary Shelley's nature, clues to our understanding of Muriel Spark. She writes of Mary, 'She was one in whom passion was very strongly restrained, due largely to the inhibiting effect of her early life in an "enlightened" and bleakly rationalistic atmosphere.'[12] Of her own childhood Muriel Spark has said, 'It is impossible to know how much one gets from one's early environment by way of a distinctive character, or whether for better or worse. I think the puritanical strain of the Edinburgh ethos is inescapable, but this is not necessarily a bad thing.'[13]

Muriel Spark's childhood and that of Godwin's daughter were no doubt very different, but the effects on their writing are similar. Mrs Spark points out that Mary was not able to reconcile the conflict in herself between the woman and the writer. She goes on,

> I believe the full play of instinct on her imagination to have been foredoomed. The passions she portrays most successfully in her novels are passions of the intellect. Where affairs of love are intended we find affairs of sentiment, and the closer we look at her individuals the further do they recede imperturbable, into prototypes.[14]

As I have indicated, I believe that Muriel Spark, too, has difficulty in conveying 'affairs of love', in allowing her instinct to influence her imagination without fear of a disorderly takeover.

The first publication of fiction by Muriel Spark was in 1951, when she won the *Observer* short-story competition with her strikingly original story 'The Seraph and the Zambesi'. She continued to write poetry, and in 1952 her first book of poems appeared, *The Fanfarlo and Other Verse*. This was followed in 1953 by a selection of Mary Shelley's letters, edited with Derek Stanford, and in 1954 Mrs Spark edited an edition of the Brontë letters. Other writers who had influenced her by this time were Max Beerbohm and Marcel Proust. Her best critical work, however, was a study of John Masefield, the Poet Laureate. She was attracted chiefly to his narrative art in both poetry and prose, and it is to this aspect of his work that she addressed herself. She was stimulated by his enthusiasm for story-telling when she visited him, and in her book commends his prose in words wholly applicable to her own: 'John Masefield's achievements in fiction are, essentially, a poet's. He uses words with the utmost sensitivity.'[15] This may have paved the way for her eventual experiment at what she has called 'a rather lazy and third-rate form',[16] bringing the realisation that a novel need not necessarily be lax and shapeless, but could be both economic and poetic.

From her Presbyterian schooling until 1952 Muriel Spark

acknowledged no religious faith, but by 1953, having thought about it for a year, she felt ready to be baptised into the Anglican Church. She was confirmed by an Anglo-Catholic bishop, however, and for several months stayed in this 'half-way house' between Anglicanism and Roman Catholicism, sometimes attending the same church as T. S. Eliot in Gloucester Road. During this time she was reading the work of J. H. Newman, and his writings were an important influence on her decision to become a Roman Catholic. She greatly admired the clarity of his style, and the thoroughness with which he had considered his own conversion. For Muriel Spark, as well as for Newman, Catholicism was not something which required strenuous intellectual adaptation, since for both of them it seems to have been the religion with which their beliefs involuntarily accorded. It was the authenticity of this attraction that they had to test, rather than the dogma of the Catholic Church itself. Mrs Spark once said, 'The reason I became a Roman Catholic was because it explained me',[17] and in the same interview she calls herself a 'Catholic animal'. But like Newman she took time over her conversion, which in her case was delayed by a dislike of Catholics themselves. 'I was put off a long time by individual Catholics, living ones, I mean. Good God, I used to think, if I become a Catholic, will I grow like them?'[18] Nevertheless, she received instruction from a monk of St Benedict's Abbey, Ealing, and in 1954 she was received into the Roman Catholic Church by Father Philip Caraman. Like Evelyn Waugh and Graham Greene, she describes her reception in a very matter-of-fact way: 'it wasn't anything huge. I'd been reading towards it for years and one wet afternoon I did it.'[19]

During the period leading up to her conversion Muriel Spark had become ill. She was trying to write a work on the Book of Job, and at the same time was suffering, like him, from a variety of afflictions which she felt obscurely to be bound up with her conversion. In fact, Mrs Spark's illness was caused in part by undernourishment, but no doubt the upheaval of her thoughts relating to her conversion added to her stress, which is vividly captured in *The Comforters*. The title is ironic, taken from Job's ineffectual friends, and emphasises the isolation she must have felt at this time. Some help was practical, however. Realising her malnutrition, Father Aegius fed her milk and biscuits when she went to Ealing for instruction, an episode recounted in *The Comforters*. Various people gave her financial help, including Graham Greene, whom she had never met. Some benefactors offered help on condition that she received medical or psychological treatment, and after her conversion she underwent Jungian therapy for six months at the hands of a priest. She was already acquainted with Jungian theory. In 1948, in an editorial in *Poetry Review*, she had referred to the collective unconscious as a fertile source of inspiration to the artist:

> Psychologists have shown how the world of dream and fantasy bears a direct relation to art; archetypal images, planetary shapes and all the experiences to which mankind is subject are inherent in the unconscious mind of the human race, and the poet, having by his very nature especial access to the rich race memory, may now identify his experience, not only with external symbols but with the infinitely more significant and accurate imagery of the psyche.[20]

In an interview in 1961, she relates this memory to her own uncanny creativity:

> even if a particular character has struck my imagination, one person I've met, I never reproduce the character in the book. It's always my experience of hundreds of characters, and also a kind of memory that I can't explain, almost as if I remember the past before I was born. As if history itself was telling me something and perhaps it's what the psychologists would call the 'racial memory' although I've no great faith in these psychological terms, but it may be something like that, that I seem to have a memory for people I've never met, or a knowledge of people I've never met. . . .[21]

It would seem that the therapy, combined with her conversion, had a liberating effect. After six months she was restored to health, and for the first time she was able to write a full-length novel.

In 1954 Alan Maclean of Macmillan, looking for new authors, asked Muriel Spark to write a novel. She was suspicious of the form, but found that her conversion had made a significant difference to her creativity: 'I wasn't able to work and to do any of my writing until I became a Catholic.'[22] She expands on this:

> The Catholic belief is a norm from which one can depart. It's not a fluctuating thing. . . . Nobody can deny I speak with my own voice as a writer now, whereas before my conversion I couldn't do it

because I was never sure what I was, the ideas teemed, but I could never sort them out, I was talking and writing with other people's voices all the time. But not any longer.[23]

From the stronghold of her Catholicism, Mrs Spark recognised her place in the scheme of things with a new assurance. This assurance, like that of Evelyn Waugh, led to a satiric view of the fallen world and her first novel, *The Comforters*, sharply delineates her former literary associates and her new Catholic acquaintances. She had frequent opportunity to observe the latter. During her illness she had moved from London to the country, and while she wrote *The Comforters* she lived in a cottage near Allington Castle in Kent, owned by the Carmelite Friars, whose centre was nearby at Aylesford Priory. Allington Castle, then as now, had a small permanent community, and was used as a retreat house. Catholics predominated, and here Mrs Spark encountered some of the characters she portrays in her first novel. Her portraits are scarcely flattering, and it would appear that their author's conversion did little to mollify her views of the faithful. A fellow Catholic convert, Evelyn Waugh, was impressed by *The Comforters*. He praised it in an address to the PEN club, and gave it a long review in the *Spectator*. Overall, the reviews of Mrs Spark's first novel were favourable, though they ranged from misunderstanding, through an uneasy awareness that more is going on than is at first perceived, to full-hearted enthusiasm. This pattern has followed the publication of each of Mrs Spark's novels: reviews have never been totally unanimous, and in almost every case a novel considered slight by one critic has been recognised as profound by another. Thus, where Frederick Karl calls her 'light to the point of froth',[24] Frank Kermode describes her as 'obsessed with her medium', a 'difficult and important artist'.[25] The problem of reconciling the frothy and serious aspects of her work is directly related to the paradox she seeks to convey – the absurdity of human behaviour in the context of a divine purpose. The means by which she relates this paradox are highly economical, and it is often this economy which is mistaken for slightness by the critic. In *The Comforters* Mrs Spark establishes a variety of themes which thread through her subsequent work: an uncomfortable allegiance to the Roman Catholic faith, an interest in reflexiveness and the manipulation of plot, a curious fascination with blackmailers and plotters. Above all, it establishes her as a writer with an exuberant interest in the potentialities of the novel form, not only for what she could say within its covers, but as a potent analogue of the world created by God as omniscient author.

The Comforters was published in 1957, the same year as the publication of *Letters of John Henry Newman*. This was a selection of letters edited jointly with Derek Stanford, and it was the last non-fiction venture by Mrs Spark. After she had finished *The Comforters* she moved back to London, although not to her former familiar areas of Kensington and Chelsea. Instead she moved to Camberwell, an unfashionable area south of the river. For many people living in Kensington Camberwell is as foreign as abroad, entailing a journey as hazardous, and it is possible that in moving there Muriel Spark was rejecting both her former associates and the environment which had comprised the literary milieu she describes in *The Comforters, Memento Mori* and *Loitering with Intent*. It was obviously a move which reduced social and pseudo-literary distractions, and it seems a fair deduction that it indicated confidence in her emotional self-sufficiency, and in her powers to utilise her ability as a serious and substantial novelist. Certainly from this time her output is prolific, and the impression is of a creature suddenly finding its element. Indeed, Muriel Spark has said of herself 'I am a writing animal . . . I write in the same way that cows eat grass. . . .'[26] In 1958 *Robinson* was published, followed by *Memento Mori* in 1959, *The Ballad of Peckham Rye* and *The Bachelors* in 1960, and *The Prime of Miss Jean Brodie* in 1961. These novels are firmly rooted in her own experience, extending back into her childhood, but viewed from a new, Catholic perspective. It was as if her faith enabled her to write by taking care of the distractions and worries that had formerly come between her perceptions of reality and her creative utilisation of them.

Mrs Spark's first two novels are largely autobiographical, and both deal with a mental crisis in the lives of their heroines. *Robinson* (1958) at first bewildered the critics. This is not surprising, since it is the most obscure and the least successful of Mrs Spark's novels. It functions as a double allegory: the psychological symbolism[27] (the man-shaped island with its cultivated headlands representing the intellect, and its interior sulphurous furnace representing the sexual and aggressive instincts) relates simultaneously to the realism of the novel and to events in Mrs Spark's own life. It works well in relation to the realistic events within the novel, but fails as a comprehensible allegorical version of the author's autobiography, since the reader is left ignorant of the reality it allegorises. There are several parallels between January Marlow and Muriel Spark. Both are writers, without husbands, and each has a young son to bring up. The 'plane crash is analogous to Mrs Spark's breakdown, and the enforced sojourn on the island to her period of recovery and return to health. In *Robinson* January realises that the crash/breakdown has affected her view of her environment, and the following passage gives a painfully accurate description of the suspicious, wary state of mind with which one views the world after a mental crisis:

> Instinctively I looked for routes of escape, positions of concealment, protective rocks; instinctively I looked for edible vegetation. In fact, I must have been afraid. And whereas, on my previous travels, I had been scenery and landscape-minded, had been botanically inclined, had been geologically enchanted, had known the luxury of anthropological speculations, I found myself now noting the practical shelter to be obtained from small craters and gulches and lava caverns. (p. 30)

The sophisticated, cultured responses have been torn away, and January sees the landscape in primitive terms of food and survival. By the end of the novel, however, she is restored to health, and is able to begin her life again at home. With *Robinson* Mrs Spark ends the relative introspection of her first two books. In her next novel, *Memento Mori* (1959), there is no character obviously resembling her, and it is as if she has progressed from struggling with her faith to applying her new-found convictions to the world around her. *Memento Mori*, of all Mrs Spark's novels, is the most lyrical and the most religiously assured, and it seems a reasonable assumption that by the time she came to write it she had achieved for herself the reconciliation she finally allows the heroines of *The Comforters* and *Memento Mori*.

While writing *Robinson* Mrs Spark had worked part-time, but the success of *Memento Mori* meant that she could at last concentrate exclusively on her own work. The critics' praise of her third novel was almost unanimous, and this was a relief because it marked for her the end of a probationary period as a novelist. Later she said of this time,

> The best thing about success is that it relieves the pressure about success. There comes an awful time for a writer when you just can't go on being promising for ever. Every book becomes one more awful milestone and you wonder whether this one will make it so that you'll be an established writer. I was really rather lucky

because my third novel, *Memento Mori*, made the breakthrough. After that no book is ever so worrying again.[28]

I get the impression that success for Mrs Spark is simply the appropriate public recognition of something she has known all along. In *Loitering with Intent* the narrator, a novelist, is struck by the thought ' "How wonderful it feels to be an artist and a woman in the twentieth century." That I was a woman and living in the twentieth century were plain facts. That I was an artist was a conviction so strong that I never thought of doubting it then or since . . .' (p. 25).

Given 'appropriate perquisites and concessions' by her teachers on account of her literary ability, Muriel Spark frequently gained prizes of books for her school by winning essay and poetry competitions. From henceforward she seems to have fostered and nourished within herself, against all adversity, a quiet knowledge of her formidable gifts. It is impressive that she did this in spite of having to earn her own living and support her young son. Even before her first novel was published, Derek Stanford noted her almost alarming confidence:

To say that Muriel regarded her gifts with expectant fondness would not be in any way an overstatement. I remember, when she lived in the Old Brompton Road, discovering her in the act of shedding a disused manuscript into tiny pieces. I asked the reason for this great precaution, and was told it was to protect the copyright of her vision against marauding poets who might come visiting her dustbin for verbal tip-offs. Was this a fantasy or a joke?

One further remark by her returns to mind. We were walking on a cold late autumn day in 1957 in Kensington Gardens, a month or so prior to the appearance of *The Comforters*. 'If only people knew how famous we were!' she observed with a sly innocent-eyed laugh. I could only bow at her kind inclusion.[29]

Later, letters relating to her work reiterate a sense of her own seriousness and importance as a writer with great talent and potential; and combined with this sense of her artistic worth is a shrewd, extremely businesslike awareness of her financial worth. Her acumen explodes the widely held notion that all artists are vague and woolly about the practicalities of life, and her letters to her former agent bristle with instructions for financial transactions, contracts, publicity. Writing from America in 1962[30] she complains that authors as yet unpublished there are offered similar advances to those that she is being paid. As her output and her fame grow, so does the need for bigger outlets and a more complex 'back-up' team, and in 1961[31] she expresses a wish to change her German publishers, because she feels that they are not sufficiently large or professional to handle her work.

After *Memento Mori* Mrs Spark wrote in quick succession two more novels set in London. These were *The Ballad of Peckham Rye* and *The Bachelors*. Together with *The Girls of Slender Means* these novels capture acutely the flavour and the moods of the city. London, in Mrs Spark's work, is not a huge, amorphous place, but very precisely defined through the viewpoint of small social groups, and she keenly traces the social nuances of both middle-class and working-class communities. This is often achieved through subtlety of dialogue, and her precision in this area is similar to that of Ivy Compton-Burnett, although the social spheres of their novels are very different. Muriel Spark has a highly accurate ear. In *Loitering with Intent* the narrator says 'My ears have a good memory. If I recall certain encounters of the past at all, or am reminded perhaps by old letters that they happened, back come flooding the aural images first and the visual second' (p. 18). This ability was exploited by Mrs Spark during the early part of her career as a fiction-writer when she also wrote radio plays for the BBC Third Programme. In 1961 a selection of these were published under the title of *Voices at Play*. Her aural memory made radio a particularly appropriate medium, and in 1962 she won the Italia Prize for Radio Drama with an adaptation of *The Ballad of Peckham Rye*. In 1962 also she had a stage play produced in London at the New Arts Theatre Club, called *Doctors of Philosophy*, a sharp and funny look at women academics and the conflicts between academe and domesticity. Play-writing did not distract her from writing novels however, and in 1961 *The Prime of Miss Jean Brodie* was first published in its entirety in the *New Yorker* magazine. This publication, famed for its urbanity, was an apt showcase for this brilliant, polished novel, and Mrs Spark was thoroughly acclaimed in America. The *New Yorker* offered her an office to work in whenever she liked, and this event heralded a change in her life. In 1962 she moved to New York, to live there for ten months of the year, while still maintaining her flat in Camberwell as a London base.

Muriel Spark calls herself a 'constitutional exile'.[32] She has lived in five countries, and her novels clearly reflect the influence of her different environments. In an interview she explained her reasons for living abroad:

> it's well known that travel stimulates a writer. First of all there are the difficulties of settling in, and then overcoming them. Obviously not being able to work for some time gives a pent-up feeling, and then one's ideas come rushing out in more of a stream, and one finally gets down to it. Also one can write against a world better.[33]

Her first environment was the Edinburgh of the 1920s and 1930s, and in an essay entitled 'What Images Return' she describes its profound effect upon her. Her first exile from the Calvinism of Edinburgh was to the comparative hedonism of colonial Rhodesia, and thence to the austerities of wartime England. Her post-war poverty did not encourage foreign holidays, but in 1961 she went to Israel for two months to research the novel which appeared in 1965 as *The Mandelbaum Gate*. The experience clearly made a deep impression on her, and in a long letter[34] to her agent she describes events which appear later in the novel: the inclination of her guide to take her to modern factories instead of the Christian shrines, and her visit to the Eichmann trial. *The Mandelbaum Gate* is Mrs Spark's longest novel to date, and it was a departure from her former succinctness. It took her two years to write, in contrast with, for example, *The Prime of Miss Jean Brodie*, which she wrote in eight weeks. The heroine is a half-Jewish Roman Catholic convert, and it is possible to see this novel as a reappraisal of its author's personality, an attempt to reaccommodate the Jewishness which for several years had been subordinated to the Catholicism.

Mrs Spark's move to America in 1962 was due to a mixture of motives. She had lived in England for eighteen years, and during that time her life-style had changed considerably. She explained in an interview with Philip Toynbee, 'One strong reason for leaving England . . . is that I'd outstripped all my old friends and associates of the days when I had no money or success. It was painful to be with them, simply because I felt like a sort of reproach to them – and they to me.'[35] In addition, her increasing fame led to a plethora of business activities and publicity which eroded the time and solitude necessary for creative writing. In 1961 Mrs Spark expressed her growing concern about this:

[I] am afraid of too many press interviews and television appearances and of my work becoming merely the administrative side of the set-up. When I have too much of this sort of stuff I get an ironic feeling and sometimes then, when I start to write, I say to myself: 'let's do a little paper work to fill in the time'.[36]

She lived in America for three years, and initially found it stimulating:

New York suits me. I like the tension and energy, being at the centre of things. It's not the literary life, or going out, or the theatre or anything like that. I've never been part of that. I hate writers talking about writing. But the vitality and stress helps me to work. And then of course I've got the use of an office at the *New Yorker* and I work office hours there. I do a day's work, 9 to 5.30.[37]

Mrs Spark's novel relating most directly to New York is *The Hothouse by the East River*, which was begun while she was living there but not published until 1973. It presents a frightening perception of the city, where the atmosphere is shown to perpetuate a sense of dislocation and insanity. New York becomes a metaphor for Purgatory, the characters trapped in a limbo of anguish and uncertainty. The setting of the novel fluctuates between wartime England and peacetime America, and paradoxically the dangers of the former are made to seem preferable to an affluent existence in a New York apartment. It is possible that Mrs Spark's life at this time, despite both wealth and fame, seemed claustrophobic compared with the poverty and vitality of her wartime existence. Her description of those days is unmistakably enthusiastic and not a little nostalgic in the context of the novel: 'In the summer of 1944 . . . life was more vivid than it is now. Everything was more distinct. The hours of the day lasted longer. One lived excitedly and dangerously. There was a war on' (p. 34). The staccato sentences accentuate their message of alertness and zest, and they contrast vigorously with the descriptions of the febrile languor in the New York 'hothouse'. Certainly Mrs Spark became disillusioned with America, and in 1966 she moved to Italy to a large apartment in Rome, overlooking the Tiber.

Since leaving England, Mrs Spark has acquired the attributes and reputation of an increasingly cosmopolitan writer. Her expatriate existence is reflected in her work, not only in its subject-matter, but also in her attitude towards it. She is cooler, even less involved, more openly an observer. Her social range has narrowed somewhat. Living in Italy, but writing in English, Mrs Spark has fewer opportunities to exploit her ear for dialogue, and thus her facility for revealing social and class differences through conversational nuances has less scope. Without simply equating the changes in her geographical location with changes in her novels, one can identify a shift, none the less, from the realistic detail of her London-based novels to the fantastic and bizarre nature of those set in New York and Italy. Mrs Spark exploits the frenetic quality of Italian life to accommodate outrageous plots, which in their context take on a reasonableness impossible in any other setting, since violence and drama have always been endemic to the English view of Italy. She admits her fascination with the Italian popular press, which furnishes her with ideas for plots: 'The journalists here are more imaginative than any I know. A combination of Latin blood and a free press. . . . I think that a lot of their energy, which might have gone into novel writing, goes into their reporting.'[38]

In Italy Mrs Spark has the opportunity to observe the importance of the cult of *bella figura*. The relationship between appearance and reality has always interested her, and her theme is often the revelation of disguise. In her first 'Italian' novel, *The Public Image*, the plot hinges on the heroine's capacity to distinguish and to choose between her self and her role as a film-star, a task made difficult because the two have been interwoven over the years by publicity and press releases. By the time she came to write *The Public Image*, Mrs Spark was herself qualified to understand the problems facing her heroine. She was successful in both artistic and financial terms, her apartment, her jewellery and her couture clothes reflecting the commercial standing of her work and contributing to her glossy image.

In her novellas, beginning with *The Driver's Seat* (1970), Mrs Spark's work takes on a harsher, more urgent tone concerned with immediate experience. The evocative, detailed descriptions, such as those of London, Edinburgh and Jerusalem, are replaced by highly economical landscapes representing an instantaneous world, where appearances replace history as the basis for negotiation, evaluation and judgement. These novellas have a hard, contingent quality, and have far less to do with moral introspection than her earlier work. They comprise a bravura, displaying coolly the complex process of fictional techniques entailed in writing a novel. *Not to Disturb* (1971) intensifies this reflexive trend, so that the emphasis of the plot is almost wholly on methods of making fictions. We are given 'scenarios', and characters themselves are allowed awareness of their abilities at role-playing or directing.

Deceptions pervade Mrs Spark's next two novels: *The Hothouse by the East River* (1973) and *The Abbess of Crewe* (1974). The latter was prompted by the Watergate scandal and, unlike some contemporary writers who confessed to feeling imaginatively overtaken by its absurdities, Mrs Spark felt no such problem. Indeed, she viewed it with complacent recognition, since the refinements of deception and the manufacture of worldly fictions have always been the subject of her novels. After a customary period to allow the initial inspiration to jell, she wrote the novel quickly, and it shares with *The Prime of Miss Jean Brodie* an amazing coherence of tone. Indeed, the two protagonists have much in common; Mrs Spark excels at conveying their controlled, authoritative megalomania, and the reader responds to their undeniable charisma. This is shared to a lesser extent by the heroine of her next novel, *The Takeover* (1976), who is also granted a certain narratorial admiration for doing things in 'style'. *The Takeover* is a long novel for Mrs Spark, and represents a departure from the five succinct novellas preceding it. Significantly, in a novel about inflation, she abandons her former stylistic thrift for a dazzling loquacity. *The Takeover* and *Territorial Rights* (1979) are concerned with current international themes – the counter-culture, inflation, terrorism – which are portrayed with a breadth of worldly wisdom. Money is a central topic in both novels, and Mrs Spark displays an impeccable knowledge of the caste-marks of the very rich.

These two novels continue the shift in her subject-matter from the religious to the secular. This is not to say that in these novels Mrs Spark is irreligious, but that they do not include details of the wearisome, day-to-day struggle of an individual aware of a soul to be lost or saved. Her range is wider, more satiric, and her targets are the larger absurdities of a godless world. Her next novel, however, reverts both to the narrator as heroine and to the London of her earlier work. *Loitering with Intent* (1981) has much in common with her first novel, *The Comforters* (1957). Its heroine, Fleur, is an established novelist, and she seems a mature version of Caroline. Fleur is relaxed, assured in the practice of her art and of her faith; and, looking back over her long life as a novelist and a Catholic, rejoices in both aspects.

Muriel Spark's success has not been without cost to her personal life. The practice of creative writing demands a ruthless allocation of priorities; its peculiar intensity means that the pursuit and maintenance of personal relationships has ultimately to remain subordinate. This is often perfectly understood by women in relation to men, and the role of the attentive and supportive wife is still common. The reverse is seldom true, however, and it is infinitely more difficult for a woman to practise her craft with the necessary singlemindedness. Muriel Spark understood the alternatives early on in her career, and made her choice accordingly. This has lost her friends. In addition to its demands on her time, her work has sometimes affected her health. In 1961[39] she complained in a letter to her agent that she was having headaches which appeared to be nervous in origin, and in another letter[40] written the same year she said that her doctor had ordered her to rest. Each novel takes a toll in terms of nervous exhaustion, and she mentions in interviews[41] that she was ill after finishing *The Mandelbaum Gate* and *The Driver's Seat*, having to complete the latter in hospital.

It is difficult to account for the intensity of Mrs Spark's motivation as a writer. She is undoubtedly an artist for whom life is crowded with potential, and through whom the ephemeral is made lasting. In *Loitering with Intent*, the narrator, a novelist, puts it better: 'When people say that nothing happens in their lives I believe them. But you must understand that everything happens to an artist; time is always redeemed, nothing is lost and wonders never cease' (p. 117).

Mrs Spark combines her rare, poetic talent with sheer Scottish industriousness, and there is also the sense of an iron determination to compensate for the losses of her early life. She married very young and, having given emotion priority over intellect, she was let down by it, and the marriage quickly failed. She missed the opportunities of going to university and of establishing herself conventionally in an academic or literary career, so that she had to find opportunities to fulfil her potential without the safety-net of a secure job. These experiences have left their mark. Throughout Muriel Spark's interviews and in the correspondence I have seen, the impression conveyed is of a matter-of-fact faith, and a ruthless singlemindedness about her work. 'People fail you' is the message of her novels, its sadness almost disguised by the elegance of its medium, almost mitigated by her assurances that God does not.

3 Religious Faith

The novels of Muriel Spark are written from a Roman Catholic standpoint, whether or not her religion is specifically mentioned. In her first two novels, *The Comforters* and *Robinson*, written soon after her conversion, religion is a central theme. Her early protagonists struggle with the demands of Catholicism in their everyday lives, and their sense of frustration and anguish comes over very clearly. By her third novel, *Memento Mori*, Mrs Spark writes more lyrically about her religion, although she never portrays it romantically, or as an instant panacea. In her later works religion is less dominant, lurking in the background as an implicit touchstone of values, flamboyantly ignored by her characters, and to their cost. By this stage Mrs Spark begins to distance herself from her characters, to record their activities with a detachment which, as I have suggested, cannot simply be accounted for by accepting her viewpoint as *sub specie aeternitatis*. In *The Takeover* and *Territorial Rights* she no longer bothers to draw our attention, as she once did, to the discrepancy between the tenets of the faith and the behaviour of the faithless. Without comment, she details what she sees around her, and, if her readers miss the satiric point implicit in her comparison between human and divine purposes, then that is merely ironic confirmation of her theme.

The novelist who is a committed Catholic faces particular artistic problems, chief of which is the relationship between faith and creative writing. As a member of the Church, allegiance is to orthodoxy; as a writer allegiance is to art. Is it possible for an imaginative artist to be both a creator and an adherent of dogma? George Orwell thought not, maintaining that usually only bad Catholics wrote good books.[1] The Catholic philosopher Jacques Maritain took the opposite view, claiming that only a Christian is properly qualified to write a novel, which he envisaged as having a lofty purpose: 'The object it has to create is human life itself; it has to mould, scrutinise and govern humanity. . . . only a Christian, nay a mystic, because he has some idea of *what there is in man*, can be a complete novelist.'[2] Maritain also denies that there need be any conflict between the views of a Christian and the demands of his work: 'Do not make the absurd attempt to sever in yourself the artist and the Christian. They are one if you really *are* a Christian, and if your art is not isolated from your soul by some aesthetic system.'[3]

This accords with Newman's remarkably confident definition of Catholic literature not as that which deals specifically with Catholic matters, but as writing including 'all subjects of literature whatever, treated as only a Catholic would treat them'.[4] None the less, some Catholic writers use the novel as a vehicle for propaganda, and they are invariably less interesting than those who feel and chart the tensions between loyalty to the Faith and the need to depict the deviations of human conduct. I am thinking of novelists as diverse as Frederick Rolfe, Graham Greene and David Lodge, all of whom express their dismay at aspects of the Catholic Church, and who chronicle the inadequacy of its relationship with the fallen world. Far from using Catholicism as a source of joyous affirmation, their attitude to their faith is critical, and Mrs Spark, also, belongs to this line of sceptical Catholic writers. Even her early, most religious novels give the impression that she is closely and critically scrutinising her faith before rejoicing in it, and her later novels scarcely mention Catholicism. Neither does she engage in Catholic polemics. There are few religious homilies in her novels, and when they do occur they are nearly always used as an ironic weapon against those who deliver them. And although the protagonists of her early novels are often converts, the actual conversion is not a dominant happening since it usually occurs before or after the events described. Mrs Spark's exposition of her faith is for the most part bleak, beset with weary frustration at complying with its rules, and intense irritation with fellow-Catholics. In *The Comforters* her attitude is summed up clearly. Two characters agree that 'the True Church was awful, though unfortunately, one couldn't deny, true' (p. 89). Mrs Spark's novels reveal both the awfulness and the truth; the lyricism with which she expresses the latter never wholly negating the misery which she implies is involved in dedication to a faith.

Catholic novelists who refuse the role of propagandist still encounter a more subtle problem, which is the presentation of evil in their work. Maritain says firmly, 'The essential question is not to know whether a novelist can or cannot depict such-and-such an aspect of evil. The essential question is from what *altitude* he depicts it and whether his art and mind are pure enough and strong enough to depict it without connivance'.[5] There is something rather chilling about this formulation. It seems to set up difficult alternatives: either the writer sees the world from a distant, bird's-eye view, surveying men's messy, sinful activities from the height of his own sanctity, or he is among them on earth, seeing at first-hand the evil he describes. Closeness entails involvement, involvement understanding, and understanding compassion; it seems an arid proposition for a novelist to depict evil without an attempt to sympathise with the deprivations (physical or spiritual) which cause it. It also seems to the layman an unchristian attitude, and it is this discrepancy between the letter and the spirit of the Church which is exploited by Catholic writers most vulnerable to censorship because of such 'connivance'. These include François Mauriac and Graham Greene. Mauriac's early novels attack the hypocrisy of middle-class Catholics, and are sympathetic to characters whom such Catholics would define as sinners. Graham Greene's canon shows compassion for the evildoer, even when this means flying in the face of Catholic doctrine. His stance has caused much disquiet amongst Catholics, and his novel *The Power and the Glory* (1940) was condemned by the Vatican. Undeterred, he continued to challenge the rules of his church. In *The Heart of the Matter* (1948) the protagonist chooses to die in mortal sin, by committing suicide. Although Greene has since said, 'The character of Scobie was intended to show that pity can be the expression of an almost monstrous pride',[6] the circumstances and viewpoint of the novel are such that his suicide comes over as a moral and generous act. It is, nevertheless, a sin according to Catholic dogma, for which the hero believes he is damned, and Greene cunningly sets up a situation where sin is shown to be morally preferable to the Church's law.

A *Burnt-Out Case* (1961) is the culmination of Greene's explicit 'connivance' with a sinner against his church, although the mood is no longer one appropriate to a burning moral issue, rather one of weariness and uninterest in the possibilities of religious truths. On his death-bed the protagonist's last words are 'This is absurd or else...', and in that sentence an entire theological argument is reduced to the words 'or else...'. It is as if Greene no longer has the spiritual energy to spare for his former persuasive rhetoric on behalf of the formal sinner. Evelyn Waugh was shocked by *A Burnt-Out Case*, and in his diary for 31 December 1960–1 January 1961 he writes,

The *Daily Mail* sent me an advance copy of Graham Greene's *A Burnt-Out Case* asking for a review for which, I suppose, they would have paid £100. I have had to refuse. There is nothing I could write about it without shame one way or the other. . . it emphasizes a theme which it would be affected not to regard as personal – the vexation of a Catholic artist exposed against his wishes to acclamations as a 'Catholic' artist who at the same time cuts himself off from divine grace by sexual sin. . . . A book I can't review.[7]

Waugh dwelt on his part in promoting Greene as a 'Catholic' artist, and on 4 January 1961 he wrote in his diary,

I wrote to Graham saying that taken in conjunction with his Christmas story, his new novel makes it plain that he is exasperated by his reputation as a 'Catholic' writer. I told him in all sincerity how deeply sorry I am for my share in this annoyance. Twelve years ago a lot of Catholics were suspicious of his good faith and I officiously went round England and America reassuring them.[8]

Waugh had obviously thought that he was protecting the spiritual reputation of his fellow-Catholic. He himself did not share Greene's dislike of being regarded as a 'Catholic' novelist, since he experienced no conflict, except at the end of his life, between what he wanted to say and what the Church wanted him to say. Waugh certainly writes from a high 'altitude'; from his lofty viewpoint he focuses on both a bygone, romantic world of English Catholicism, and the divine world to come. This present, fallen, mundane universe compares unfavourably with past and future glories, and Waugh keeps his distance by satirising its shortcomings, although clearly he feels no hope of correcting them.

Muriel Spark's presentation of evil is also free from 'connivance', and the altitude from which she depicts it is high and the atmosphere rarefied. Her attitude to her characters' sinful behaviour is uncompromising. Sin is sin, and it is not mitigated by circumstances, although, with God's grace, it can become an unexpected source of virtue. Unlike Graham Greene, she does not build up a situation where an understanding of a character's personality goes half-way to explain and possibly to excuse an evil action. The chief method by which she maintains her detachment is by keeping her people at a distance. She does not share an author's love for his characters defined by John Bayley as 'a delight in their independent existence as *other people*, an attitude towards them which is analogous to our feelings towards those we love in life; and an intense interest in their personalities combined with a sort of detached solicitude, a respect for their freedom.'[9] This emphasis on freedom and independence of character – the weight and impetus of the novel depending on this – is clearly far from Mrs Spark's view, which is of a being bound, willingly or unwillingly, by the ordinances of God; and, by analogy, bound as rigidly by the restrictions imposed by the novelist. For all their liveliness and verve, her people are denied the freedom of a human individuality, since we are made constantly aware that their choices and actions function merely as components in both a novelistic and a divine plot. And, because their roles are predetermined, it is part of Mrs Spark's economy not to give us a psychological, interior view of them, nor to penetrate their thoughts and motives, since in her view this might elicit our sympathy for their personalities at the expense of our attention to the dynamics of the plot. In her middle work particularly, she seldom gives us sufficient information about her characters for us to feel an easy sympathy with them. Very few of them have families, or a sense of belonging somewhere, and there is no sense of experiential growth; at best her people fulfil what is shown to be their already latent potential through circumstances beyond their control. It is as if this social and emotional isolation enables Mrs Spark to get down to essentials; the impression given is that the careful nurturing of sympathy for the foibles and nuances of personality is an indulgence when the state of the soul is what needs to be considered.

All the same, it is an attitude which seems uncharitable and somewhat incongruous in a novelist who is a Christian. Christopher Ricks, in what I think is a mistaken interpretation of *The Public Image*, nevertheless puts his finger on the nub of the problem: ' "Merciless" the reviewers have always said. Leave aside the question of why something which is a vice in life becomes a virtue in literature, but why fabricate characters at whose expense you can then exercise your mercilessness?'[10] It is not so much that Mrs Spark deliberately invents characters simply in order to express her contempt for them; rather that they embody her view of the fallen world. She too is part of that world, and thus her detachment becomes a method of coping with self-contempt as well as a method of survival. In his diary for 1962 Evelyn Waugh includes some notes made 'some twelve years' previously. One of them reads,

Abjuring the realm. To make an *interior* act of renunciation and to become a stranger in the world; to watch one's fellow-countrymen, as one used to watch foreigners, curious of their habits, patient of their absurdities, indifferent to their animosities – that is the secret of happiness in this century of the common man.[11]

Mrs Spark's work suggests that this is how she too views her fellow men. Isolated from her family and contemporaries by her successive exiles and by her unique talent, a sense of separation has left spaces in her novels which have been accounted for by an aesthetic of detachment. She does not feel she has to provide emotional directives for the reader. In an interview with Frank Kermode she said, 'Things just happen and one records what has happened a few seconds later.'[12] This is an odd description of the creative process, and is in a way a denial of it, since in her terms it would be a kind of sacrilege. Dry-eyed, 'one records what has happened', leaving God to pass judgement, and to extend mercy if he thinks fit.

Muriel Spark's conversion to Roman Catholicism was a significant turning-point in her life and in her career as a writer. Conversion can mean, of course, either the adoption of a belief in God where none previously existed, or the shift of belief from one religion to another. In each case it involves a new perspective on the world arising from a strong sense of personal conviction in the rightness of such a viewpoint. William James says, 'To say that a man is "converted" means . . . that religious ideas, previously peripheral in his consciousness, now take a central place, and that religious aims form the habitual centre of his energy.'[13] Before her conversion Mrs Spark's central motivation was her intense desire to be a writer, and she cared too much to succeed. In an interview she says, 'I didn't feel that I could grasp a subject and achieve it, because it mattered too much. As a Catholic I feel that nothing matters all that much. . . . And so I was released in a liberated way.'[14] By 'nothing' Mrs Spark presumably means 'nothing worldly', and this realisation paradoxically allowed her to achieve what she no longer considered of paramount importance. She was able to write from a new sense of security, and she has called her religion 'a norm from which to depart'.[15] In addition, the Catholic faith gave formal expression to what she already believed, and thus sanctioned it. Like Newman, who was her greatest influence, Mrs Spark believed in angels and demons, and had a sense of divine control behind phenomena. Like Newman, too, she retained an awareness of childhood as extraordinary. In an interview she tries to describe this strangeness: 'I had the impression of childhood itself being unusual, life being unusual. . . . I think children are capable of almost mystical experiences. . . . I think that one had intimations of immortality.'[16] Newman, writing about his childhood when he was a young man, recalls, 'I thought that life might be a dream, or I an Angel, and all this world a deception, my fellow-angels by a playful device concealing themselves from me, and deceiving me with the semblance of a material world.'[17]

In his perceptive book about the Oxford Movement, *Oxford Apostles*, Geoffrey Faber comments on the function of dogma for Newman – initially Calvinistic, later Roman Catholic:

> In his old age he was still substantially the child who walked with God at Ham and dreamed that his brother-angels were hiding themselves from him. All the resources of his intellect were employed throughout his life to protect that dream from destruction.
>
> That was the function of dogma in his mind. It was the solidest buttress he could find to the aethereal constructions of his childhood.[18]

The security of religious dogma gave Newman confidence. Faber goes on to note Newman's greater gregariousness as a Roman Catholic priest, and points out that 'in the Roman Catholic system he enjoyed the maximum of protection and the maximum sense of community with his kind.'[19] Muriel Spark did not at first experience this sense of community: 'I didn't like some of the Roman Catholics I met awfully much, and they put me off for a long time. There were some nice people but I didn't like the way they drummed things in.'[20] But eventually their common ground became more important than her irritation with individual Catholics: 'Yet now I think I would prefer to live with Catholics because I have not got to be so much on my watch with them. There are so many basic things in common and a kind of basic trust.'[21]

Part of Mrs Spark's annoyance with some Roman Catholics stemmed from their attitude to her as a convert, an attitude clearly portrayed in *The Comforters*. There is perhaps a sense in which the convert can never feel as 'Catholic' as a person born into that faith, and reminders of this difference can be painful. On the other hand,

Donat O'Donnell refers to Mauriac's 'envy of converts . . . for whom Catholicism had been a matter of choice'.[22] This is an important distinction between the 'cradle' Catholic and the convert. For the former, faith is familiar, unquestionable, given. It is not primarily an intellectual matter, since its precepts are practised and accepted before they are understood. For the convert, Roman Catholicism is alien, questioned and acquired. If an emotional or instinctive feeling for the religion is the basis of its attraction, this has to be tested by instruction and understanding. Truth, for a convert, implies rejection of a former, inadequate set of tenets. For a 'cradle' Catholic truth implies acceptance, a passive, less rebellious role, involving no such dramatic demonstration of belief. It is not difficult to understand Mauriac's envy, which is not so much of the convert's choice, but of the fact that his move to Catholicism has had to be motivated by an intense belief amounting to a spiritual necessity, and is a matter of positive conviction.

The stimulus of conversion, and the desire to pass on newly realised truths, account for many Catholic novels written by converts, and in England the majority of Catholic novelists have been converts rather than 'cradle' Catholics. Even if the subject-matter is not specifically religious, the author's new faith may give an unusual slant on secular events. In a short story, 'The Portobello Road', Muriel Spark describes a brutal murder, and the reaction of one of the victim's friends: 'Kathleen, speaking from that Catholic point of view which takes some getting used to, said, "She was at Confession only the day before she died – wasn't she lucky?" ' (*Collected Stories I*, p. 30). That is a shocking sentence, hardly softened by Mrs Spark's unusually generous admission that this angle of vision 'takes some getting used to'. It is also a very economic way of looking at things, a view of the world *sub specie aeternitatis*, where even sin provides the potential for salvation. In an article on Muriel Spark's work, Derek Stanford wrote,

Cardinal Newman once remarked that a Christian picture of the universe is almost necessarily a poetic one, and this notion so took Miss Spark's fancy that she once copied out his words in a book of essays on him which she presented to me. I remember that, in a conversation we once had, Miss Spark remarked how literally 'economic' the Catholic cosmography struck her as being. The skies and the aether were populated with legions of spirits – instead of being just so much waste space.[23]

This 'poetic' or metaphoric vision of the world pervades Mrs Spark's work. She sees the external visible world not as distinct from the spiritual world, but as a sacramental manifestation of it. In an article on Proust, she describes this as 'the idea that the visible world is an active economy of outward signs embodying each an inward grace'.[24] Nothing, in this view, is arbitrary. Each event or action has its place in the divine pattern, which may not necessarily be evident at the time. Throughout her novels, Mrs Spark displays her awareness of what a character in *The Prime of Miss Jean Brodie* perceives as 'a sense of the hidden possibilities in all things' (p. 106). Even sin is not wasted. In *The Bachelors* Ronald Bridges says, 'The Christian economy seems to me to be so ordered that original sin is necessary to salvation' (p. 90). This is the idea of the fifteenth-century carol 'Adam lay y-bounden', which celebrates the original sin which necessitated our redemption:

> Ne had the apple taken been,
> The apple taken been,
> Ne had our lady
> A-been heavene queen.

> Blessed be that time
> That apple taken was.
> Therefore we moun singen
> Deo Gratias.

In Mrs Spark's novels, one might say, particularly sin is not wasted, since her evil characters sin spectacularly and to great purpose. This paradox, which she has called in another context 'that deep irony in which we are presented with the most unlikely people, places and things as repositories of invisible grace'[25] recurs in her work. In *The Girls of Slender Means*, for example, we keep our spiritual expectations on pure Joanna the vicar's daughter, and our secular ones on the sexy Selina. But, ultimately, it is the recognition of evil in Selina that is to Nicholas a means of grace, since he is aware that 'a vision of evil may be as effective to conversion as a vision of good' (p. 180). In *The Bachelors*, also, the theme is the ironic discrepancy between human desires and divine will, and it emphasises that in our partial understanding of the divine purpose, we do not always pray for the right things. Patrick Seton is on trial for fraud, and his pregnant mistress, Alice, prays for his acquittal, unaware that if freed he intends to murder her. 'It's a test of God' (p. 206), says Alice, and when Patrick is found guilty she says immediately, 'I don't believe in God' (p. 239). Her belief is irrelevant to God's purpose. Her life is saved, and before the birth of her child she will be married to another man. Her participation in the pattern is completed in ways she has never contemplated.

The paradoxical necessity of evil as a means to good is particularly evident in Mrs Spark's early novels. In *The Comforters* Mrs Hogg is shown to be essential to Caroline's spiritual progress, just as Robinson and Tom Wells are necessary to January in their different ways. In *The Prime of Miss Jean Brodie* Sandy Stranger sleeps with Teddy Lloyd, who is married and a Roman Catholic. Sandy incidentally becomes interested in Catholicism: 'Her mind was as full of his religion as a night sky is full of things visible and invisible. She left the man and took his religion and became a nun in the course of time' (p. 165). In *The Mandelbaum Gate* Miss Rickward's malevolence towards Barbara is, ironically, beneficial to her, the forged baptismal certificate enabling rather than preventing her marriage to Harry. And Frederick's histrionic suicide in *The Public Image*, designed to finish his wife's career, does just that, the irony being Annabel's profound sense of liberation as she is released from the bonds of her 'image'. Above all, these stories illustrate a religious design superimposed on worldly events. Nothing is gratuitous: everything is shown, by the end of the novels, to be part of the divine plan. What may have seemed to the reader (and to the characters) appalling or unnecessary evil during the course of the narrative is revealed at the end as necessary and redemptive.

In Muriel Spark's fiction, as in that of Graham Greene, we are often shown that the way to God is not always through conventional channels, and an especial stress is put on the notion that there is a kind of divine satire being practised when God mocks the rational expectations of those committed to piety. This is the theme of Mrs Spark's short story 'The Black Madonna'. Raymond and Lou Parker are a childless Catholic couple living in a New Town. Their local church has a fine statue of the Virgin Mary, which is carved from bog oak and known as the Black Madonna. The statue acquires a reputation, since prayers addressed to it are frequently granted. The Parkers, of working-class background, affect liberal views which, in Lou's case, are shot through with snobbery. They choose to live in a council flat, despise television, and feel superior to their neighbours. They often entertain two black Jamaicans, Henry and Oxford, who

work with Raymond, introducing them to all their friends to show
how tolerant and broadminded they are. Their tolerance, however,
undergoes a severe test. Jealous of her sister's fecundity, Lou decides to
pray to the Black Madonna for a baby. Her husband, suspecting Lou
of merely wanting to test the powers of the Madonna, advises her to
consider whether or not she really wants a baby after all. ' "You have
to be careful what you pray for", he said. "You mustn't tempt
Providence." . . . "I don't see why I shouldn't have a baby", said
Lou' (*Collected Stories I*, p. 67). They are delighted when Lou becomes
pregnant. But, to their horror, the baby is black. Raymond suspects
that one of the Jamaicans is the father, but it transpires that there is
negro blood, generations back, in Lou's family. Nevertheless, the
neighbours gossip, and Lou and Raymond decide to have the baby
adopted, even though tests prove that it is undoubtedly their own. The
story ends with a subtle moral summary of their action:

'We've done the right thing', said Lou. 'Even the priest had to
agree with that, considering how strongly we felt against keeping
the child.'
'Oh, he said it was a good thing?'
'No, not a *good* thing. In fact he said it would have been a good
thing if we could have kept the baby. But failing that, we did the
right thing. Apparently there's a difference.' (p. 76)

'The Black Madonna' is a sharp attack on hypocrisy, on those
whose outward attitudes of piety bear no relation to their inner lives.
The Parkers' religious practices and their self-consciously liberal
views are maintained merely to impress their less high-minded
friends. Mrs Spark shows the frailty of their principles when put to the
test. Throughout the story, Lou is shown weaving little scenarios to
suit herself, regardless of reality. Her sister Elizabeth is widowed with
eight children, and lives in an East London slum. Lou, before her
pregnancy, sends her a small sum of money each week, and builds up
a picture of her sister as a frugal and deserving recipient of her
charity: 'Sending off the postal order to her sister each week she had
gradually come to picture the habitation at Bethnal Green in an
almost monastic light; it would be bare but well-scrubbed, spotless,
and shining with Brasso and holy poverty' (p. 60). When she visits her
sister for the first time in nine years, Lou sees that she is casual and
feckless, and her house smelly and dirty. Lou is very upset, because it
reminds her too vividly of what she herself has managed to escape

from, and the precarious newness of her respectability. When Henry, who is black, says that Elizabeth has a 'slum mentality', Lou's racial prejudice surfaces. 'Lou was thinking wildly, what a cheek *him* talking like a snob. At least Elizabeth's white' (p. 64). Mrs Spark excels at conveying character through nuances of diction, and Lou is very aware of the importance of language as a reflection of values. Early in the story an unsophisticated acquaintance calls their black friends 'darkies' and is immediately corrected. ' "You mean Jamaicans", said Lou' (p. 58). But by the end of the story, in her anger at bearing a black child, Lou forgets the euphemisms, and says what she really thinks. 'Imagine it for yourself, waking up to find you've had a black baby that everyone thinks has a nigger for its father' (p. 76).

In 'The Black Madonna', Mrs Spark carefully leaves realistic, natural explanations available for the apparently supernatural happenings: the psychological factors of infertility and pregnancy; the 'throwback' from Lou's negro ancestor. The force of the plot, however, comes from the idea of divine purpose rather than unrelated coincidence. 'God is not mocked' is the underlying text of the story, and, indeed, Elizabeth's semi-literate letters remind Lou that 'God is not asleep' (p. 74). God asserts his absoluteness in a highly mischievous way, and the fact that the baby is a genuine, if unwelcome miracle is not even acknowledged by the Parkers in their panic and anger.

In her first two novels Mrs Spark describes the problems and difficulties of adjusting to Roman Catholicism through the experiences of her protagonists, both Catholic converts. Caroline Rose and January Marlow epitomise what we come to recognise as a typical Sparkian heroine – a sharp, intelligent, independent thinker, not given to displays of emotion, and, if a Catholic, reluctantly so, with an abhorrence of Catholic cliques and their attendant prejudices. These early characters experience painful conflicts between their own desires and the exhortions of their newly adopted Church (particularly those concerning charity and chastity) and they react by over-intellectualising. In *The Comforters* we are told that 'Caroline was an odd sort of Catholic, very little heart for it, all mind' (p. 231). In *Robinson* the heroine progresses, as it were, to realising the dangers of a purely intellectual approach to Catholicism, which Mrs Spark implies is one sort of denial of faith. Significantly, Robinson, the owner of the island January is stranded on, cultivates only the headlands, ignoring the potential fertility of the rest of it, and living mainly on imported food from tins. The cultivation of the intellect at the expense of the instincts is a source of disquiet to January, and she begins to reject the repressive function that Robinson represents. Although he too is a Catholic, he is very suspicious of January's desire to worship, and he confiscates her rosary so that she should not teach it to his foster-son.

> 'I am thinking of Miguel', he said. 'I wish him to grow up free from superstition.'
> 'To hell with you', I said. 'There's nothing superstitious about the rosary. It's a Christian devotion, not a magic charm.'
> 'All those Hail Marys', he said.   (pp. 102–3)

In his absence, January overrides his wishes and when Robinson returns she says with great confidence in the rightness of her action, 'I am happy to say I have taught the child the rosary' (p. 176).

The character in direct contrast to Robinson is Tom Wells, who is interested in the occult, and who appeals to the pagan, superstitious side of January's nature. He also represents her own sexuality and aggression, and near the end of the novel he tries to murder her in an underground tunnel, but she manages to escape. This fight is analogous to the struggle at the end of *The Comforters*, where Mrs Hogg (a symbol of grossness and sensuality) nearly drowns Caroline in the river. Like January, Caroline escapes, but both encounters are terrifying, and the sense of almost overwhelming forces is very powerfully conveyed. In 'My Conversion' Mrs Spark briefly mentions the clash between sex and religion in her own case. She says,

> It's a bit of a nuisance not being able to have a sex life if you're not married, but it has its advantages if you have a vocation, a mind obsessed with a certain subject or a job to do in life. It's not so easy for people less obsessed. The best thing then is to get married if you can.[26]

For the heroines of Mrs Spark's first two novels sexual deprivation is more than 'a bit of a nuisance'. Caroline has to stop sleeping with her boyfriend, Laurence, who, being a lapsed Catholic, is more understanding than most. 'He reflected how strangely near impracticable sexual relations would be between them, now that

Caroline thought them sinful. She was thinking the same thing'
(p. 104). But sex being taboo, it becomes distorted and threatening.
Having given up Laurence, Caroline becomes obsessed with Mrs
Hogg, who represents for her a sickening carnality:

> Caroline realized that she had been staring at Mrs Hogg's breasts
> for some time, and was aware at the same moment that the
> woman's nipples were showing dark and prominent through her
> cotton blouse. The woman was apparently wearing nothing
> underneath. Caroline looked swiftly away, sickened at the sight, for
> she was prim; her sins of the flesh had been fastidious always.
>
> (p. 29)

Later, in *The Bachelors*, Mrs Spark is far more light-hearted when
dealing with the problem of Catholicism and sex. We are given a
hilarious description of an Irish Catholic, Matthew Finch, guarding
against what he calls his 'weakness', which is going to bed with girls.
He eats raw onion before a date, 'For he had found that the smell of
onion in the breath invariably put the girls off, and so provided a
mighty fortress against the devil and a means of avoiding an occasion
of sin' (p. 52). Unfortunately for Matthew the girl from whom he
defends himself likes the smell of onions, so he succumbs.

Charity is more difficult to practise than chastity in Mrs Spark's
novels. She makes her Catholic protagonists find their fellow-
Catholics almost intolerable, and Laurence warns Caroline that 'you
have to pick and choose amongst Catholic society in England, the
wrong sort can drive you nuts' (p. 24). Mrs Hogg certainly shows
herself adept at needling Caroline. Skilfully, she perceives the
convert's insecurity and plays on it:

> 'Mm . . . I know your type', Mrs Hogg said, 'I got your type the
> first evening you came. There's a lot of the Protestant about you
> still. You'll have to get rid of it. You're the sort that doesn't mix.
> Catholics are very good mixers. Why won't you talk about your
> conversion? Conversion's a wonderful thing. It's not *Catholic* not
> to talk about it.'   (pp. 29–30)

This fiendish convolution increases Caroline's tension, and we are
given realistic descriptions of the neurosis from which she suffers.
After talking to Mrs Hogg, Caroline 'had a sudden intense desire to
clean her teeth' (p. 31) and after Mrs Hogg visits her she sprays her

room with 'a preparation for eliminating germs and insects' (p. 208). In *The Bachelors* Ronald Bridges makes himself practise charitable thoughts, which do not come easily, about a group of weak and corrupt people:

> He forced upon their characters what attributes of vulnerable grace he could bring to mind. He felt sick. Isobel is brave ... Marlene is handsome, Tim is lovable, Ewart Thornton is intelligent ... Martin Bowles is considerate to his mother. (p. 121)

Nowhere does Mrs Spark convey the impression that the Catholic religion brings easy, automatic spiritual grace, and she treats with fury Catholic characters who are complacent about the benefits of their religion. When Caroline goes on a retreat to the Pilgrim Centre of St Philumena, she meets Catholics who are self-satisfied and self-righteous. Their conversation is almost a parody of genuine suffering overcome by genuine faith. One pilgrim says smugly, 'The wonderful thing about being a Catholic is that it makes life so easy. Everything easy for salvation and you can have a happy life' (p. 39). This view is not shared by Mrs Spark's protagonists. Time and again their religion involves suffering and sacrifice, not necessarily on a grand, exalted scale, but in small and niggling ways which are far more vexatious to the spirit.

Mrs Spark's satire is not restricted to obviously unpleasant Catholics. Sir Edwin and Lady Manders, in *The Comforters*, are extremely well-meaning; they employ Catholic maids, endow Catholic centres, and Sir Edwin makes frequent religious retreats. Their motives are of the highest, but as Mrs Spark chronicles events in their lives she reveals the gaps between the motives and the effectiveness of their actions. Helena, Edwin's wife, used to employ Mrs Hogg, and now lives in terror of her. Instead of confronting her, and accusing her of both moral and literal blackmail, she makes excuses for the woman's malevolence, and fobs her off by finding her new employment. Helena's excuse is, 'one tries to be charitable' (p. 208), and it is only Caroline, in her clear-sighted way, who recognises her cowardice for what it is and says to her 'Don't you think ... that you misconstrue charity?' (p. 210). Sir Edwin's religious retreats make him noted for his piety, but he is incapable of dealing with family crises as they arise. Consequently he is seldom asked to do so, and his religion remains a separate and ineffectual part of his life.

Other people's attitudes to Catholicism form part of the cross borne by Mrs Spark's Catholic characters. For many it is an extremely provocative subject, and in *The Mandelbaum Gate* Barbara Vaughan listens to an attack on the gullibility of Catholics:

> '*So* many Catholics won't listen to any other religious writings. It's killing. And the things they swallow themselves ...'
> This was nothing new to Barbara; ever since her conversion she had met sophisticated women who, on the subject of Catholicism, sneered like French village atheists, and expected to be excused from normal good manners, let alone intelligence, on this one subject.' (p. 288)

In *The Bachelors* too, people are rude to Ronald about his religion. At a luncheon party his hostess declares that she is 'anti-Catholic', and goes on,

> 'But I don't mean I'm anti *you*', said Marlene. 'You're sweet.'
> 'Oh, thanks.'
> 'There's a distinction', Tim pointed out, bright with tact, 'between the person and their religion.'
> 'I see.' Ronald attended closely to his potatoes. (p. 46)

This distinction between a person and his religion irritates Ronald, and when asked how he feels about something 'as a Catholic' he loses his temper: ' "Don't ask me", Ronald shouted, "how I feel about things as a Catholic. To me, being Catholic is part of my human existence. I don't feel one way as a human being and another *as a Catholic*" ' (p. 83).

The psychological nature of *The Comforters* and *Robinson* indicates that their heroines expressed Mrs Spark's own uncertainties and difficulties concerning her new religion. Having endured the demands of charity and chastity, the desire to over-rationalise their faith, and the idiosyncracies of fellow-Catholics, her protagonists are allowed to achieve some peace of mind. Caroline copes with the sneers of her former acquaintances, and the threat of Mrs Hogg. January comes to terms with the stresses of her religion in relation to her personality, and finds a balance between over-controlling her instincts and totally submitting to them. At the end of the novel, she comments on the transformation this experience has wrought:

Even while the journal brings before me the events of which I have written, they are transformed, there is undoubtedly a sea-change, so that the island resembles a locality of childhood, both dangerous and lyrical. . . . And sometimes when I am . . . feeling, not old exactly, but fusty and adult – and chance to remember the island, immediately all things are possible.   (p. 186)

This passage has echoes of *The Tempest*:

> Nothing of him that doth fade
> But doth suffer a sea-change
> Into something rich and strange.
> (I.ii.397)

But it is the final line which is the most illuminating, making January's experience essentially a religious one by its association with the line from St Matthew's gospel '. . . with God all things are possible' (Matthew 19:26). Although Caroline and January are restored to health, the form of *Robinson*, in particular, works against such a conclusion. There is a contradiction between the novel's highly formal, allegoric structure and its deeply emotional content. The symbolism is irritating, because through it Mrs Spark seems to be straitjacketing the pain and anger of her personal experiences in a tight literary genre; the three-to-three relationship of symbol and events, its patness, is too neat to be a convincing account of a breakdown and return to health. Perhaps Mrs Spark felt that a realistic treatment of her illness, conversion and adjustment to Catholicism would be too like *The Comforters*, or maybe *Robinson* was a distancing device, rendering anguish into a case study. Whatever the reason, a pattern has been imposed, rather than realised, and, for all her trials, January's recovery to spiritual well-being is less credible than that of Caroline Rose.

By her third novel, *Memento Mori*, Mrs Spark has acquired far greater confidence both in the expression of her faith, and in her handling of the novel form. She has overcome her suspicion of the novel's transparency. Instead of overloading it with devices such as allegory, symbolism, parody of popular plots, as if these things demonstrated a worthiness of serious attention it would not otherwise merit, she has capitalised on its more conventional attractions, such as suspense and characterisation. She can afford to become simpler since the central theme of *Memento Mori* is so extraordinary: her belief in the supernatural as an aspect of reality, and her use of it as a dynamic moral force. For Mrs Spark the physical world is irradiated and made significant by its spiritual dimension. In *The Mandelbaum Gate* she has a priest say in a sermon that 'there is a supernatural process going on under the surface and within the substance of all things' (p. 214), a statement of faith which is at the heart of her work. She accounts for this world in the light of another, and she seeks to unify the two. One of the methods she uses to achieve this is the introduction of supernatural elements into her novels: an invisible tapping typewriter, a mysterious voice on the telephone, a demonic–angelic visitant, a medium in contact with the dead, a group of souls in purgatory. The majority of these other-worldly occurrences are in her early novels, since these are most concerned with the exposition of her faith. The strange happenings are usually presented without the narrator's explanation, and are initially as puzzling to the reader as to the characters. A rational explanation is temptingly dangled before us, almost but not quite fitting as a comfortable solution to an uncomfortable problem. Thus, Caroline's voices and tapping typewriter might be hallucinations, until we are told by the narrator that Caroline's own realisation of an omniscient author writing about her is, in fact, true. The telephone voices in *Memento Mori* might be a series of malicious calls, but the first suggestion that the caller is 'Death himself' (p. 157) comes from one of the sanest and most reliable characters in the novel. It is not specifically verified by the narrator, but the whole emphasis of the novel favours the supernatural rather than the naturalistic explanation. Dougal Douglas might be merely an Edinburgh arts graduate and a trouble-maker, but he is surrounded by numerous references to his 'angel–devil' (p. 36) appearance, his vestigial horns, his dislike of crossing water, and his own and others' diabolical claims for him. Patrick Seton we are told is a genuine medium, although capable of intensifying his performance with the aid of drugs, and using his powers for purposes of fraud. The characters in *The Hothouse by the East River* are indubitably supernatural, having been killed by a V-2 bomb in 1944, long before the main action of the novel.

So the rational answer will not suffice, since Mrs Spark blurs the boundaries between the tangible and intangible, and it is difficult to say where one ends and the other begins. She herself sees nothing remarkable in this. She says, 'I haven't a strong sense of distinction between natural and supernatural; I think we're all involved in the supernatural world.'[27] Her characters, however, seldom share this kind of vision, and the ways in which they cope with the intrusion of the supernatural is a measure of their insight and moral growth. Those who recognise and accept the possibility of the apparently irrational, who realise the existence of a world not explicable in human terms, find the experiences liberating. Their idea of reality is enlarged to include heaven and hell. Those who cannot cope with the new, extraordinary and often frightening experience remain trapped in their narrow rational world. The perceptions offered to the characters within the novels are available to the reader. By the end of a novel such as *Memento Mori*, for example, it is plain just how confined and inadequate is the realism set up at the beginning of the narrative. Death is originally seen in terms of old age, illness, nursing homes, funerals and obituaries in *The Times*. As the story progresses, the message 'Remember you must die' leaps out from the novel with a particular relevance to each reader, and the more practical aspects of death are rendered totally peripheral. Thus the novel becomes, very literally and very seriously, a meditation on death, a genuine *memento mori*.

In *The Comforters* the supernatural was merely one of many weird happenings; in *Memento Mori* it is the pivot of the plot. A variety of old people are telephoned by a mysterious caller who says 'Remember you must die' (p. 2), and our interest is focused on the wide range of responses to this message. As Peter Kemp points out,[28] the reaction of the characters to the telephone call varies according to their moral bearing. Most of the people telephoned are practised at blotting out the thought of death and refuse to accept the evidence of their old age. Dame Lettice 'thought, How shaky my writing looks! Immediately, as if slamming a door on it, she put the thought out of sight' (p. 110). Instead of altering their perspective on life and preparing themselves for death, the characters continue to behave as they have always done, even though old age dictates the scaling-down of their activities. Thus eighty-seven year old Godfrey Colston (whose first name sounds like a sharp little Sparkian pun), formerly adulterous, now pays women to show him their stocking-tops. He is also extremely mean, having refused to pay nursing-home fees for his wife's lifelong servant and companion (which he could well afford), and splitting matches into two with a razor-blade, in order to get two boxes for the price of one. Percy Mannering, an aging poet, engages in a pathetic literary feud over the reputation of Ernest Dowson. This feud culminates in a battle of mock-epic proportions — two elderly gentlemen jabbing

feebly at each other's walking sticks – and is one of Mrs Spark's
funniest pieces of writing. Another character who behaves as if she
were at the height of her powers is Tempest Sidebottome. She is on the
management committee of a hospital, and she is tolerated because she
demonstrates 'to the point of parody' (p. 120) the shortcomings of an
old-fashioned approach to hospital management. The members of the
committee all know where they are with her: 'everything beginning
"psycho-" or "physio-" Tempest lumped together, believed to be the
same thing, and dismissed' (p. 119). In the geriatric ward of the
hospital the old ladies, like their wealthier counterparts, also have
fantasies and devices to cope with their old age. Granny Barnacle, a
former newsvendor, makes a new will out once a week; 'she would
ask the nurse how to spell words like "hundred" and "ermine" '
(p. 9). Godfrey's sister, Dame Lettie, plays a 'real will-game' (p. 10),
designed to keep her relatives in suspense. After her death, twenty-
two different wills are found among her papers, dated over forty
years. Her obsession with wills, however, is not related to an
awareness of her mortality, but a way of trying to exercise power over
her heirs, who largely ignore her existence. Dame Lettie is a noted
penal reformer and prison-visitor, and through her Mrs Spark
satirises the worldly reformist dreams of those who steadfastly neglect
to change themselves first. As soon as she receives her telephone-call
reminding her that she must die, Dame Lettie thinks a criminal is
responsible, and publicly regrets that flogging has been abolished. The
absurdity of all these actions is heightened in the context of the
telephone-message, since they seem to the reader, if not to the
characters, extraordinarily petty in the light of the Four Last Things:
death, judgement, heaven and hell.

In contrast, Mrs Spark includes in *Memento Mori* three characters
who are able to contemplate dying with comparative equanimity.
Two are Catholic converts, and the third is a retired policeman, who
is not given any specific religious belief. But they have all, in different
ways, developed a philosophy of living which includes the acceptance
of death, and the message 'Remember you must die' holds no terror
from them, being merely the statement of a fact with which they have
already come to terms. Charmian Colson is not particularly devout,
but she reacts very calmly to the message which causes some of the
other characters to slam down the 'phone and call the police:

'Oh, as to that,' she said, 'for the past thirty years and more I have
thought of it from time to time. My memory is failing in certain

respects. I am gone eighty-six. But somehow I do not forget my
death, whenever that will be.' (p. 139)

Her former companion, Jean Taylor, became a Catholic after her
employer, 'really just to please Charmian' (p. 44), but is now greatly
fortified by her faith. She exists in a public geriatric ward, where the
elderly women are called 'Granny' indiscriminately. Jean is of a
different class and background from the other patients, and the
experience of the public ward is at first terrible and humiliating. But
she comes to terms with it through the application of her faith:

> After the first year she resolved to make her suffering a voluntary
> affair. If this is God's will then it is mine. She gained from this state
> of mind a decided and visible dignity, at the same time as she lost
> her stoical resistance to pain. (pp. 10–11)

Although Jean is not given a specific message, she finds her own
memento mori in a new group of patients in states of advanced senility
who are moved into the ward. But she hears of the telephone-calls
from those of her former acquaintances who, from mixed motives,
continue to visit her. Dame Lettie confides her fears about 'that
distressing sentence' (p. 35). Jean suggests, 'Perhaps you might obey
it' (p. 35). Later she says, 'It's difficult . . . for people of advanced
years to start remembering they must die. It is best to form the habit
while young' (p. 36). Dame Lettie ignores the implications of what
Jean is saying by assuming that her mind is wandering.

It is Henry Mortimer, the retired police-inspector used to
evaluating evidence, who comes to the correct conclusion: 'In my
opinion the offender is Death himself' (p. 157). He sees death, not so
much in terms of the Four Last Things, but as a vital ingredient to the
full appreciation of life:

> If I had my life over again I should form the habit of nightly
> composing myself to thoughts of death. I would practise, as it were,
> the remembrance of death. There is no other practice which so
> intensifies life. Death, when it approaches, ought not to take one by
> surprise. It should be part of the full expectancy of life. Without an
> ever-present sense of death life is insipid. (p. 166)

In contrast to the world of petty jealousies and ancient feuds indulged
in by most of the other characters, his retirement with his wife is

placid and happy. He enjoys gardening, fishing and sailing, and the visits of his grandchildren. Mrs Spark builds up a picture of the Mortimers as an ordinary, suburban couple, who, being neither self-important, nor melodramatic, accept their evident mortality with ease. The characters who hold themselves in the highest esteem, such as Dame Lettie, seem affronted at the thought of their lives ending.

Memento Mori is a pessimistic novel in that no one is shown to accept the implications of the message, and to improve his life as a result of it. In both *The Comforters* and *Robinson* the heroines grow in grace having undergone a disturbing experience; in this novel the supernatural disturbs, but not for the better, rather intensifying the worst traits of the characters who are frightened by it. Those who are not alarmed have already come to terms with the fact of their mortality, and Mrs Spark strengthens her case for the feasibility of this practice by making its participants neither wholly virtuous, nor even, in the case of Henry Mortimer, religious. The point of the novel is that the inevitability of death should imbue everyday actions with significance: those with faith are reminded that they will be accountable to God for their earthly- life; to those without faith, it gives, paradoxically, an even stronger motivation to live fully and well, since they believe that they alone are responsible for their own redemption of existence from absurdity. There is no doubt, however, that the argument of this novel is primarily for a religious appreciation of life. It is one of Mrs Spark's most certain affirmations of her faith, and within it references to religious beliefs are made either in a tone of heightened, lyrical prose, or in the lucid, utterly authoritative style that is usually reserved for indisputable fact. For example: 'In the course of the night Granny Trotsky died as the result of the bursting of a small blood-vessel in her brain, and her spirit returned to God who gave it' (p. 52). Each fact, the name of the patient, her death and its cause, and the return of her spirit to God, is given the same narrative weight, having the status of truth rather than of pious hope or personal opinion. At the end of the novel, the characters' fatal diseases are listed in the cold, clinical terminology of a gerontologist, but in the final paragraph Mrs Spark returns to Jean Taylor, the person who has epitomised throughout the Christian approach to death. The tone changes from one of detachment to one of total endorsement, and the final words of *Memento Mori* beautifully reiterate its theme: 'Jean Taylor lingered for a time, employing her pain to magnify the Lord, and meditating sometimes confidingly upon Death, the first of the four last things to be ever remembered' (p. 246).

The Ballad of Peckham Rye, which succeeds *Memento Mori*, seems at first to be in total contrast to it, since God is scarcely mentioned, an absence reflecting the spiritual wasteland of Peckham. This void is not filled by any expression of narratorial regret, and the only religious voice in this novel comes from Nelly Mahone, an elderly lapsed Catholic, who stands on street-corners declaiming the Bible. Her words are meaningless to passers-by, because they are familiar with her role of a dotty old vagrant, but in fact they act as a relevant commentary on the activities of the protagonist, Dougal Douglas. He is an ambiguous creature, half-angel, half-devil, whose function is to act as a catalyst on the inhabitants of Peckham Rye. Dougal is amoral, but like the telephone-call in *Memento Mori* he acts as a stimulant, disturbing the spiritual torpor of Peckham, and in some cases making people aware of the narrowness of their lives. The words 'ignorant' and 'immoral' permeate the book; used indiscriminately by the characters about each other to describe a range of activities from adultery to incorrect grammar, they are shown also to be an accurate description of Peckham life. Most people in the novel are snared in sterile personal relationships, but where Dougal is able to show them the possibility of freedom the result is not always liberating in a congenial sense. Their lethargy erupts into violence, nervous breakdowns, even murder. No one is able to use Dougal's disruption advantageously, just as no one in *Memento Mori* benefited from the reminder of death, and after his departure from Peckham the characters slide back into their former apathy. Mrs Spark does not allow the novel to rest there, however. In the final paragraph of the novel we are offered a vision, momentarily perceived, whereby the dreariness and immorality of Peckham is transcended. In a description of the Rye we are told that one of the characters 'saw the children playing there and the women coming home from work with their shopping-bags, the Rye for an instant looking like a cloud of green and gold, the people seeming to ride upon it, as you might say there was another world than this' (p. 202). This is a view of Peckham, transfigured, that is not shown in the novel, but this brief and poetic statement is pointedly made the final comment. Mrs Spark insists that what we have seen is not the total sum of man's condition, and that Peckham exists also in an external context.

This perception of God's immanence in the secular world informs Mrs Spark's work. She sees the physical aspect of reality as a significant manifestation of God's purpose (however imperfectly this is understood), and not merely as a lumbering, failed ethereality. In her Proust article she expressed her distrust of a dualistic attitude portrayed in some Christian creative writing 'which . . . in an attempt to combat materialism, reflects a materialism of its own; this takes the form of a dualistic attitude towards matter and spirit. They are seen too much in moral conflict, where spirit triumphs by virtue of disembodiment. This is really an amoral conception of spirit.'[29] In the same article she commends 'a sacramental view of life which is nothing more than a balanced regard for matter and spirit'.[30] In *The Mandelbaum Gate* Barbara Vaughan realises that 'Either the whole of life is unified under God or everything falls apart' (p. 308) and the failure of her characters to achieve this unity is the theme of Mrs Spark's early novels. They either refuse to accept that everyday reality has a divine dimension, or they concentrate on isolating the spiritual, rejecting callously the material aspects of God's creation. The spiritualists in *The Bachelors* exemplify the latter approach, which, taken to extremes, is highly dangerous. Patrick, who is a medium, is shocked by Alice's desire for marriage, 'as if he were a materialist with a belief in empty forms' (p. 174). For Patrick marriage is not sacramental, but equated only with. man-made laws, which are dismissed as being contrary to the life of the spirit. His contempt of matter enables him to plan Alice's murder as if he were doing her a favour: 'I will release her spirit from this gross body' (p. 174). He influences another of his mistresses, Mrs Freda Flower. Three months after her husband's death, unable to reconcile the idea of physical decay and spiritual survival, she has him disinterred and cremated, because 'since she had come to believe so ardently in Harry the spirit, she simply could not let him lie in the grave and rot' (p. 26).

Patrick is, of course, extremely malevolent, but in this novel even so apparently innocuous a state as bachelorhood is considered graceless. Matthew Finch, who has been educated by the Jesuits, is particularly concerned at being single, the more so since he is unable to remain celibate: ' "I'm afraid we are heretics," he said, "or possessed by devils. . . . It shows a dualistic attitude, not to marry if you aren't going to be a priest or a religious. You've got to affirm the oneness of reality in some form or another" ' (p. 89). Matthew does this by marrying Alice. For Ronald Bridges, who suffers from epilepsy, it is more complex. The ancient beliefs in both the prophetic power and the demonic possession of epileptics are implied in the way Ronald functions in the novel. He is a graphologist, and as a detector of frauds he is placed in a clinal relationship with Patrick, a perpetrator of them. His powers of acute perception, analogous to those of a medium, are related to the illness from which he suffers: 'he became, at certain tense moments, a truth-machine, under which his friends took on the aspect of demon-hypocrites' (p. 9). At the end of the novel Mrs Spark stresses not only his disgust with his fellow men, but also his self-disgust:

> He slept heavily and woke up at midnight, and went out to walk off his demons.
> Martin Bowles, Patrick Seton, Socket.
> And the others as well, rousing him up: fruitless souls, crumbling tinder, like his own self which did not bear thinking of. But it is all demonology, he thought. . . . (p. 240)

Throughout the novel we are shown that a close look at his fellow men does indeed resemble the study of demons, and that Ronald himself is not exempt from demonic characteristics; his own imperfect nature is externalised by his epilepsy, which acts as a kind of metaphor for it. Nevertheless, he is a Christian, and in his mind he seeks to accommodate these evils within the province of God. This is made particularly difficult for him because his epilepsy has, demon-like, frustrated his desire to become a priest. Consequently he is told,

> '. . . you never had a vocation.'
> 'How do you know?'
> 'Because, in the event, you can't be a priest . . . But you can do something else.'
> 'I could never be first-rate.'
> 'That is sheer vanity' – it was an old priest speaking – 'you were never meant to be a first-rate careerist.'
> 'Only a first-rate epileptic?'
> 'Indeed, yes. Quite seriously, yes', the old priest said. (pp. 6–7)

Again, this is a 'Catholic point of view which takes some getting used to'.[31] Ronald does try to accept his epilepsy and incorporate its implications into his way of life. He decides not to marry a girl who attempts to shelter him from its consequences, and when Matthew asks him if he wants to marry, he says, 'No . . . I'm a *confirmed* bachelor' (p. 80). The religious pun emphasises that Ronald begins to see the possibility of a vocation in his epilepsy and in his single state, even though Mrs Spark makes it clear that such acceptance does not come easily to him.

Nowhere else in her work does the author so clearly convey the frustrations of a person in whom an awareness of God coexists with such soul-sickening depression. The murky atmosphere of *The Bachelors* is of deception, emotional and moral expediency, of people battening on one another with leech-like singlemindedness. And although he is unshakably a Christian, Ronald cannot wholly transcend a mood of deep pessimism at what he sees around him:

> His melancholy and boredom returned with such force when he was alone again in his flat that he recited to himself as an exercise against it, a passage from the Epistle to the Philippians, which was at present meaningless to his numb mind, in the sense that a coat of paint is meaningless to a window-frame, and yet both colours and preserves it: 'All that rings true, all that commands reverence, and all that makes for right; all that is pure, all that is lovely, all that is gracious in the telling; virtue and merit, wherever virtue and merit are found – let this be the argument of your thoughts.' (p. 116)

The point is carefully made that Ronald is not able to use this passage as spiritual comfort, but as a 'mere charm to ward off the disgust, despair and brain-burning' (p. 117). Nevertheless, Mrs Spark implies that regardless of Ronald's motives, the attempt to counter despair with biblical truths is the right course of action. The most cogent acknowledgement of faith comes not from Ronald, but from the narrator on his behalf. After a particularly bad night involving demonic thoughts and culminating in a seizure, Ronald decides to go to Confession the next morning, 'to receive, in absolution, a friendly gesture of recognition from the maker of heaven and earth, vigilant manipulator of the Falling Sickness' (p. 122). This puts Ronald's epilepsy within God's control, and Ronald has to understand his affliction as part of God's purpose for him. But *The Bachelors*, unlike *The Comforters*, does not end with a climax of evil overcome. Patrick is put out of harm's way, and Alice is married to someone else, but Ronald's struggle goes on. His triumph is not in defeating his demons in favour of God, but in accepting the fact that throughout his life they will coexist, and then, with faith, getting on with life as best he can.

With *The Bachelors* Mrs Spark ends her series of early novels on the specific subject of the Roman Catholic faith. She returns to it later, in

The Mandelbaum Gate, but there her attitude is different, her outlook wider. Her early work (with the exception of *The Ballad of Peckham Rye*) details the problems of conversion, and goes on to chronicle the benefits but also the miseries of those who live according to the precepts of Catholicism. Taken together, they form a coherent account of the convert's experience, totally unromanticised, and thus all the more convincing when an individual achieves a measure of hard-won grace, however small. In these novels Mrs Spark's moral certainties are inextricable from the teachings of her church. The characters who make genuine attempts to understand and live by its laws are granted narratorial endorsement: Caroline Rose, January Marlow, Jean Taylor and Ronald Bridges are all shown to be unquestionably right in their efforts, however halting, to apply their faith to their lives. Those who live outside the Church are shown to be wrong, however well intentioned, and the interest of the plots lies in the contrast between eternal and temporal perspectives on the world. Mrs Spark's early Catholics do not question the tenets of their faith, as later protagonists do, and neither is there any narratorial doubt expressed in these novels. Their central theme is simply that the doctrine of the Roman Catholic Church is true. Their plots recount the ways in which people accommodate or deny this awkward fact in their twentieth-century lives.

4 Secular Influences

The publication of *The Prime of Miss Jean Brodie* in 1961 brings a change of manner and emphasis in Mrs Spark's work. This novel and its successor, *The Girls of Slender Means* (1963), are works of great authority. Their certainty of tone is similiar to that of *Memento Mori*, but they are motivated by a darker and more pessimistic vision. The action of her early novels was centred on the Roman Catholic faith, towards which her characters aspired. Later novels, however, lose their insistence on the force of the other world, and its positive place in the sometimes seedy realities of this one. Supernatural events no longer occur, and the revelation of the spiritual aspects of reality depends on our eliciting an oblique morality from the narrative without necessarily being given a specific creed from which to take our bearings. Mrs Spark concentrates on portraying evil as it is manifested through the actions of an individual, or through the godlessness of contemporary society, leaving it to the reader to postulate a moral system thus violated. We are given hints that Catholicism provides such a system, but it is no longer shown to be an enabling factor or a saving grace.

Mrs Spark's sixties novels, from *The Prime of Miss Jean Brodie*, to *The Public Image*, are subject to a moral viewpoint, but only in *The Mandelbaum Gate* is this allied with that of a Catholic protagonist. Characters in the three other novels are converted in various ways as a result of events described, but the narrative emphasis is on the events themselves. The moral perspective is blurred, moreover, by the ambiguous stance of the narrator towards the protagonists, and we see Mrs Spark's increasing complicity with their participation in the sins their predecessors struggled to resist. In *The Prime of Miss Jean Brodie* (which I examine in a later chapter) both Jean Brodie and Sandy Stranger play God; Nicholas Farringdon's life is a muddle of self-deception until he is suddenly and shockingly enlightened; Barbara

Vaughan gives her love-life priority over her religious obligations, and Annabel Christopher conspires with her image-makers. They do not remain in these states though, because at this stage in her canon, Mrs Spark's moral implications are still dynamic; and the characters achieve resolutions which are ironic in the light of their actions, indicating that God is still the 'vigilant manipulator' even though he is kept behind the scenes.

The Girls of Slender Means is set in a girls' hostel in London in 1945. The title has a triple meaning, referring not only to the economic and moral poverty of most of the girls, but also to their 'vital statistics', aspects which are all skilfully interwoven in the plot. The moral polarities of the novel are symbolised by Selina Redwood, who is beautiful and evil, and Joanna Childe, who is 'healthy looking' (p. 21) and good. Attracted in different ways to each of them is a young man called Nicholas Farringdon, who has written a book entitled *The Sabbath Notebooks* calling for anarchy and atheism. He is trying to get the book published, and persuades Jane, the publisher's assistant, to write a letter (purporting to be from Charles Morgan) saying he is a genius. The main feature of Nicholas's character is its constant indeterminacy: he is a bisexual who vacillates between extremes such as pacifism and joining the army, committing suicide and 'an equally drastic course of action known as Father D'Arcy' (p. 63). The climax of the novel is the moment when Nicholas commits himself, almost involuntarily, to Christianity, and thence to martyrdom in Haiti.

Mrs Spark uses Selina to stress the point that appearance and reality are often at odds. She is very beautiful, and cultivates a cool, languid demeanour by repeating two sentences, twice daily: 'Poise is perfect balance, an equanimity of body and mind, complete composure whatever the social scene. Elegant dress, immaculate grooming, and perfect deportment all contribute to the attainment of self-confidence' (pp. 59–60). She epitomises both the loveliness and the savagery Mrs Spark attributes to the hostel girls at the beginning of the novel. Initially the word 'savage' seems shocking and inappropriate, but as the novel progresses we realise its peculiar aptness:

The May of Teck girls were nothing if not economical. . . .
    'I thought you said she was in love with the boy.'
    'So she was.'

'Well, wasn't it only last week he died? You said he died of
dysentery in Burma.'

'Yes I know. But she met this naval type on Monday, she's
madly in love with him.'

'She can't be in love with him,' said Nicholas.

'Well, they've got a lot in common she says.'

'A lot in common? It's only Wednesday now.'   (p. 121)

While Selina's boyfriend is away in the army, she enjoys herself as
much as possible in the austerity of post-war London. She goes to
night-clubs, sometimes borrowing from another girl a beautiful
Schiaparelli evening-dress, which is much sought after and lent out to
slim people in return for soap or sweet-coupons. Selina likes weak
men, because they are less possessive, and sleeps with several of them,
accepting gifts of black-market luxuries. Nicholas becomes obsessed
with Selina, and has an affair with her, endowing her not only with
clothing-coupons, but also with moral qualities that she does not
possess or even aspire to. They make love during summer nights on
the flat roof of the hostel, accessible only to slim girls who are able to
squeeze through a small lavatory window. The reader is reminded of
Selina's extreme self-obsession when she abandons someone who gets
stuck in the window, naked and yelling, in order to go to her room at
precisely six o'clock to repeat her two sentences on poise. Mrs Spark
makes it clear throughout the novel that it is the calculated quality of
Selina's selfishness which is so appalling.

Joanna Childe is her antithesis. She is an Anglican vicar's daughter
who is training to be an elocution teacher. Having sacrificed a
potential love-affair with a curate through muddled idealism, she left
the country for London, but is different from the majority of the girls
at the May of Teck club. Another hostel girl recognises that the
difference lies in her complete lack of self-absorption: 'Jane was
suddenly overcome by a deep envy of Joanna. . . . The feeling was
connected with an inner knowledge of Joanna's disinterestedness, her
ability, a gift, to forget herself and her personality' (pp. 142–3).
Joanna's choice of poetry for her elocution lessons is significant. She
prefers devotional or primarily emotional works; poetry for Joanna,
particularly its sensuous and moving qualities, takes the place of sex:
'The sensation of poetry replaced the sensation of the curate' (p. 25).
Mrs Spark utilises the elocution lessons by placing apt quotations in
juxtaposition with certain actions in the novel. The poetry acts as a
commentary on the plot – sometimes ironic, sometimes prophetic.

When the superficiality of the hostel girls' emotions are described, Mrs Spark follows the dialogue with lines from 'The Ancient Mariner', which Joanna just happens to be declaiming:

> Like one, that on a lonesome road
> Doth walk in fear and dread,
> And having once turned round, walks on,
> And turns no more his head;
> Because he knows a frightful fiend
> Doth close behind him tread. (p. 121)

We are reminded that a spectre of evil is ever present, however flippant and innocent the girls may seem. Similarly, after reading with the others an irate notice to the girls from the chairwoman of the hostel committee – 'The Committee regrets that the spirit of the May of Teck foundation has apparently so far deteriorated . . .' (p. 6) – Joanna murmurs: 'He rageth, and again he rageth, because he knows his time is short' (p. 8). This amuses the girls, who do not recognise the reference to the devil and do not realise Joanna's seriousness. Joanna takes literally the point that 'the spirit of the May of Teck . . . has deteriorated' and the line acts as a pointer to the reader. Like the unexploded bomb which lies in the garden of the hostel, events are smouldering towards an explosion. Of all the girls, only Joanna is aware of the potential danger of their moral poverty.

When the bomb does finally explode it ruptures a gas-main and sets the lower floors of the hostel on fire. Several of the girls, including Selina and Joanna, are trapped at the top of the building. The small lavatory window is the sole exit, but only those girls who are very slim can take advantage of it. Selina and two other girls slip easily through the window and escape. While the remainder are desperately waiting for firemen to rescue them, Selina returns to the hostel through the window, watched by Nicholas, who calls out to her that it is impossible to help anyone. To his horror, he sees her coolly returning through the window a second time holding the Schiaparelli dress like a limp body in her arms. As she sees Nicholas she says, 'Is it safe out here?', and he replies, 'Nowhere's safe' (p. 161), realising the extent and tenacity of evil. He crosses himself involuntarily as protection against Selina and the diabolical element she embodies, and also as an assertion of an alternative reality to the one she represents. Joanna, bearing witness to that alternative, recites the evening psalm of the day while the girls wait in terror: 'Except the Lord build the house: their labour is but lost that build it' (p. 164). She is last up the firemen's ladder to freedom, and the building collapses killing her before she can escape.

The most frequently quoted poem in *The Girls of Slender Means* is 'The Wreck of the Deutschland' by Hopkins, and this echoes the theme of the novel. Joanna's recitation in the face of disaster is analogous to the nun's praying in the sinking ship. She too, 'rears herself to divine/Ears'[1] and she too represents the apparently pointless waste of life and innocence which is endemic in the world and which is difficult to understand in association with the idea of a loving and caring God. Mrs Spark does not claim to have the answer. She simply shows us the effect of the fire on Nicholas. Afterwards Jane says, 'It was hell', and he says, 'I know.' Jane's colloquialism does not conceal Mrs Spark's statement of what she sees as fact, which Joanna, having a religious perspective, also appreciated. When Nicholas tells her father, 'She had a sense of Hell', he is surprised:

> I've never heard her speak morbidly. It must have been the influence of London. I never come here, myself, unless I've got to. I had a curacy once, in Balham, in my young days. But since then I've had country parishes. I prefer country parishes. One finds better, more devout, and indeed in some cases, quite holy souls in the country parishes. (p. 172)

Mrs Spark is unable to resist a jibe at this: 'Nicholas was reminded of an American acquaintance of his, a psycho-analyst who had written to say he intended to practise in England after the war, "away from all these neurotics and this hustling scene of anxiety" ' (ibid.).

After the episode of the fire Nicholas goes with friends to join the crowds celebrating VJ night. He observes a seaman stab a woman silently in the park, but is unable to draw attention to this because of the confusion in the cheering crowd. Instead, he makes the enigmatic gesture of putting in the seaman's blouse the forged letter Jane had composed in praise of his work. It is a gesture not explained by the narrator, but to the reader it symbolises a rejection of his former life. Years later, after his death, Jane and a friend discuss Nicholas's religious conversion:

> 'Well, I always like to think it was Joanna's example. Joanna was very High Church.'

'But he wasn't in love with Joanna, he was in love with Selina. After the fire he looked for her all over the place.'

'Well, he couldn't have been converted by Selina. Not converted.'

'He's got a note in his manuscript that a vision of evil may be as effective to conversion as a vision of good.' (p. 180)

Both Selina's action and Joanna's death are seen by Nicholas as aspects of hell, and belief in hell entails a belief in heaven. Beyond this implication, however, there is no religious or moral summing-up of the narrative. As in 'The Wreck of the Deutschland', there is no attempt to rationalise or to explain the catastrophe, nor, in worldly terms, is there any apparent justice which might act as its own commentary on preceding events. Selina goes off with a 'crooner', and the murdering sailor is left free. Nicholas is murdered several years later. Joanna loses her life in the fire. Even a tape-recording of her voice is wiped by accident for 'economy reasons'. Nicholas is angry about this, but Mrs Spark implies that the 'economy reasons' (p. 168) are not only those of wartime shortages. Joanna's recorded voice has gone because even a reminder of her is now redundant. She has served her purpose, which, it is suggested, is that of a witness to Christianity. Having done this, she is no longer needed, sheer length of life being accounted less important than its purpose. Nicholas dies a Christian martyr, transformed unintentionally by Selina. Her fate is simply being herself, although there is evidence that she perceives, and is horrified by Nicholas's new awareness of her character when he eventually finds her after the fire. Nevertheless, there is no mention of retribution; Selina too has served her purpose.

In *The Girls of Slender Means* the religious emphasis of earlier novels is shifted. Joanna is of course a Christian, but she is not a typical Sparkian Christian, beset with scepticism, and apt to ask awkward questions. And, paradoxically, this makes her less convincing. She is meek, accepting, and entirely unselfish, and obliquely Mrs Spark suggests that through her endless capacity for self-sacrifice she is emotionally destroyed long before the fire kills her. Nor can Nicholas be taken to exemplify Christian or Catholic values. The narrative concentrates almost entirely on his life before his conversion, and in fact it is only hinted that he becomes a Roman Catholic. The chronicle of events in *The Girls of Slender Means* becomes significant only by an awareness that it is unified by faith, and this awareness is left largely to the reader to supply. We are given hints towards this

end, particularly by the relevant juxtaposition of Joanna's quotations
with the novel's action, but God is displaced as a central narrative
concern.

In her next novel, *The Mandelbaum Gate*, Mrs Spark reverts to her
earlier examination of God as crucial to the life of her protagonist, but
her treatment of Catholicism is different. It is not merely a
reaffirmation of her faith but a re-examination of it, almost as if to
counter an increasing pessimism about the role of religion in everyday
life. By the time she came to write *The Mandelbaum Gate* Mrs Spark
had been a Catholic for over ten years, and the novel is written from
the mature and experienced viewpoint of a practitioner rather than
that of a probationer. It echoes *Robinson* in its theme of the heroine's
self-examination, but this time the allegorical element reinforces
rather than detracts from it. Her heroine, Barbara Vaughan, is a half-
Jewish Catholic convert, who falls in love with an archaeologist called
Harry Clegg. Her Jewishness (which she associates with her sexuality)
enhances her love-life, but her Catholicism causes a conflict between
her desires and those sanctioned by her church. Her lover is a non-
Catholic and she is forbidden to marry him unless he is able to get an
annulment of his former marriage. This crisis between two aspects of
her personality, symbolised by her Jewishness and her Catholicism,
causes Barbara to travel to the Holy Land to seek to re-establish her
identity, since Jerusalem too embodies both the Old Testament and
the New. While she is there she discovers that her Jewish blood
prevents her from legitimately making a pilgrimage to the shrines in
Jordan. For Barbara, an avid pilgrim, this is a genuine deprivation,
just as the celibacy imposed by her religion is a deprivation of a
different kind. The theme of *The Mandelbaum Gate*, as personified in
Barbara and epitomised by the city of Jerusalem is division and the
means of unity. Unlike the earlier novels, this one does not offer the
Catholic faith as a painful but unqualified solution. Other factors force
themselves into consideration, such as a Jewish heredity and culture,
the demands of sexual love and marriage, and the vital need to become
a wholly integrated person at ease with both inherited and adopted
faiths. *The Mandelbaum Gate* is an exceptional novel in Mrs Spark's
canon, and it seems to represent, in both personal and literary terms, a
bid for freedom.

By this I mean that it is possible to associate Mrs Spark with her
heroine, Barbara Vaughan, and to see the novel as a fictionalised

version of a similar quest in the author's experience. This does not
entail a precise correlation of motives between author and heroine, but
the narrative does suggest an attempt by Mrs Spark to assert some
kind of independence of faith, or at least to accommodate aspects of
her nature formerly made dormant by adherence to its laws.
Whatever the relevance of this attempt to Mrs Spark's own life, it is
certainly true of her heroine. In all Mrs Spark's novels up to *The
Mandelbaum Gate* sexual and spiritual fulfilment are made
incompatible. The enjoyment of one entails the destruction of the
other. Barbara's viewpoint is different in that she sees sexual
deprivation as a distortion or suppression of her true personality. She
feels very keenly that her English, virginal, spinsterly appearance is a
deception, and Mrs Spark repeatedly draws an analogy between
Barbara's existence and that of a nun: 'Barbara described bits of her
love-affair with Harry Clegg, and her life before that, how it now
seemed that she had been living like a nun without the intensity and
reality of a nun's life' (p. 302). Viewed by her conventional relatives,
Barbara realises that 'to them, she was a settled spinster of thirty-
seven . . . one who had embraced the Catholic Church instead of a
husband, one who had taken up religion instead of cats' (p. 36). And
when she receives a letter from the headmistress of the school where
she teaches, who has learnt of her intention to get married, we are told
that it had the tone of a 'neurotic Mother Superior to a nun with a
craving to get out'. The metaphor is made literal when Barbara is
rescued from a convent in Jordan, where, for political reasons, she is
in danger. The danger to Barbara is more than political, however, and
the location of her liberation is symbolic. After a dramatic escape in
the middle of the night, the metaphor is again stressed: 'Barbara lay
awake, marvelling at her escape from the convent. . . . She thought,
it's like the enactment of a reluctant nun's dream . . .' (p. 172).
Finally, as if the message might not be crystal clear it is spelt out: 'It
was not any escape from any real convent, it was an unidentified
confinement of the soul she had escaped from' (p. 174). This sentence
is interesting in that the narrator actually denies the realistic episode,
which undoubtedly, in the context of the novel, really happens. This
denial serves to emphasise the metaphoric implications of Barbara's
deliverance, the inappropriateness of labelling her as 'nun-like' as if
that took care of her whole personality. Barbara's liberation is
described in terms of 'escape', whereas in Mrs Spark's earlier novels
liberation is defined in terms of submission within the confines of the
Faith. *The Mandelbaum Gate*'s exceptional theme stresses its departure

from the norms previously established in her work. The early novels, for all their soul-searching, are demonstrations of faith with an implied QED at the end of each one. The protagonists struggle, but they never actually succumb to the temptation of questioning the rightness of their religion. In *The Mandelbaum Gate* the heroine not only finds the practice of her religion almost intolerable, as did Caroline Rose and Ronald Bridges, but actually doubts its truth and relevance to her own life.

This is shown in the description of Barbara's love affair. Having broken the rules and slept with Harry, Barbara is obliged to confess and rep·nt in order to be reconciled with her church. This she cannot do: 'It is impossible to repent of love. The sin of love does not exist' (p. 45). This is a feeble excuse in the eyes of the Church, and it is also a strange, unfamiliar statement coming from Mrs Spark. The claims of human love are given precedence (albeit temporarily) over the claims of faith, and this is a reversal of her former priorities. The Church, however, persists, and a compromise is reached: 'Barbara went so far as to repent that she could not repent of the forbidden love-making, and as is the plain expectation of all Christians she got the benefit of the doubt on the understanding that she put an end to the sex part of it' (p. 44). This does not solve the problem, however, since Barbara is tormented by alternatives of marrying outside the Church, or of giving up Harry altogether. While in Jerusalem, she ponders on this dilemma, and also on whether to take the risk of visiting Jordan to see the Holy Places. This would be extremely dangerous because of her Jewish blood, and she is persuaded not to go. In Mrs Spark's novels, however, unexpected incidents change the course of events. Barbara attends one day of the Eichmann trial, and is appalled by the discrepancy between the reality of the past massacre and the 'dead mechanical tick' (p. 187) of the legal discourse in which it was now being expressed. Having heard the testimony of Eichmann, the distancing of the horror by the impersonal language, Barbara decides, almost unconsciously, to go to Jordan regardless of the risk. That evening she tells Harry by telephone that she will marry him anyway, with or without the blessing of the Church. We are not told precisely how the Eichmann trial changed Barbara's mind on these two vital decisions, indeed Mrs Spark makes clear that it was not a precise process. But we are shown that what horrifies her is Eichmann's pose as an unthinking automaton obeying bureaucratic instructions: 'The man was plainly not testifying for himself, but for his pre-written destiny. He was not answering for himself or his own life at all, but for an imperative deity named Bureau IV-B-4, of whom he was the High Priest' (p. 189).

Earlier in the novel we learn that Barbara, a mixture of Jew, Gentile and Catholic, seeks to define her identity to herself. Later we meet Abdul Ramdez, an assured and sympathetic Arab, who rejects both Arab and Israeli propaganda, and who delights in disinterested action unrelated to causes or movements: 'this was something Abdul could never make his middle-class Arab acquaintance understand – how it was possible to do things for their own sake, not only possible but sometimes necessary for the affirmation of one's personal identity' (p. 90). As the clues accumulate we realise that for Barbara the Eichmann trial has presented in an acute form the danger of shifting one's own responsibilities and decisions onto an impersonal force, whether it be the Church, or a political party or a national movement. The trial reveals an abyss that she herself has to confront. Eichmann's mindless obedience makes it imperative for her to exercise her own moral judgement, in the hope that God will ratify her decision. But the essential point of *The Mandelbaum Gate* is that Barbara makes up her own mind, prior to the Church's opinion, believing this process to be essential to establish her own identity. She feels the need to acknowledge the Jewish part of her before acknowledging the Catholic, and then to try to unite the two. We have already seen Barbara struggling to fuse ancient and modern, at the beginning of her visit to Israel. When she is taken on a guided tour she wants to see the ancient religious sites, but her guide wants her to admire the factories and blocks of flats that signify the modern state. She says, 'I'm really interested essentially in the Holy Land', only to be told by her guide 'This is the Holy Land' (p. 20). Similarly she has to accommodate both her old and new religions. During a conversation with a Jewish archaeologist 'She then remarked, without relevance, that the Scriptures were specially important to the half-Jew turned Catholic. The Old Testament and the New, she said, were to her – as near as she could apply to her own experience the phrase of Dante's vision – "bound by love into one volume" ' (p. 22). Nothing is irrelevant in Mrs Spark's novels, and the analogy of the Bible, incorporating both Jewish and Christian doctrine, one prefiguring the other, represents for Barbara the unity she is trying to achieve.

It is through Freddy Hamilton that Barbara begins to accept the liberating, rather than the nullifying, properties of paradox. Freddy is an English diplomat she meets in Jerusalem, a quiet, reserved man, extremely well-mannered and given to writing formal verses to his hostesses instead of thank-you letters. He has had a brief, unhappy marriage, and is now dominated from a distance by a bullying and possessive mother. Extreme emotion of any kind alarms Freddy, and he neutralises the effect of a foreign country by employing the phrase 'quite absurd' to any extremes which are potentially threatening. Freddy assumes that English people abroad all share his attitudes, and he makes the mistake of implicitly criticising the Jews to Barbara. He is highly embarrassed when she reveals that she is half-Jewish, and when he realises that she does not therefore quite fit into the English-spinster category in which he had mentally placed her. She disturbs him still further when, on a later occasion, she states that she will never see her fiancé again if Rome does not annul his former marriage. Freddy, who is 'afraid she had some tiresome deep conviction' (p. 15) remonstrates with her about the extremity of this action, whereupon Barbara turns on him and furiously quotes from the Book of the Apocalypse: 'I know of thy doings, and find thee neither cold nor hot; cold nor hot, I would thou wert one or the other. Being what thou art, luke-warm, neither cold nor hot, thou wilt make me vomit thee out of my mouth' (p. 16). Freddy defends himself by mentally labelling this 'quite absurd', but Barbara's words are an accurate summary of what is wrong with Freddy's character. We realise that the words make a deep impression on him, because, staying with friends in Jordan, he reuses the quotation at them – this time because they are opposing the idea of Barbara's pilgrimage to Jordan on account of her Jewish blood. Suddenly Mrs Spark allows Freddy to deviate from his well-mannered, pacifying image, and during the subsequent two days he realises his capacity for impulsive action and intensity of feeling.

Freddy's first impulsive action is to destroy letters he has written to his mother, her companion, and their doctor in Harrogate. The letters from his mother and her companion, Benny, have been increasingly fractious, each complaining bitterly of the other, and Freddy has found answering them a tedious duty. He then decides to rescue Barbara from the convent, and to disguise her as an Arab servant in order that she may continue her pilgrimage. This midnight adventure stimulates them both. Barbara, realising that Freddy 'had regained some lost, or forgotten element in his nature', begins to understand that paradox may not be incompatible with wholeness and unity: 'She had caught a bit of Freddy's madness and for the first time in this Holy Land, felt all of a piece, a Gentile Jewess, a private-judging Catholic, a shy adventuress' (p. 173). In her Arab disguise, Barbara attends Mass at the Church of the Holy Sepulchre, and listens to a sermon which is an important 'set-piece' in the novel. It is preached by an English priest to a group of pilgrims, and his text is from the Epistle to the Hebrews: 'We have an everlasting city, but not here; our goal is the city that is one day to be' (p. 210). The custodians of the church are hostile to the priest for preaching, since there are other pilgrims waiting to enter for Mass, and the sermon is given against a framework of their annoyance. There is no narratorial affirmation of the sermon, but, when Mrs Spark is writing about what she considers to be eternal and important truths, her prose takes on a tone of sheer authority and authenticity which has no need of narratorial guidelines to make it convincing. So it is here. The priest warns the pilgrims against fraudulent and false shrines, and stresses the impossibility of total accuracy over religious sites: 'If you are looking for physical exactitude in Jerusalem it is a good quest, but it belongs to archaeology, not faith' (pp. 213–14). We are reminded that Barbara's fiancé is an archaeologist, and that his methods of finding truth are different from her own. Echoing Newman's motto, the priest talks of the unity that Barbara longs to perceive in the Holy Land and, by analogy, within herself:

> For there is a supernatural process going on under the surface and within the substance of all things. In the Jerusalem of history we see the type and shadow of that Jerusalem of Heaven that St John of Patmos tells of in the Apocalypse. . . . This is the spiritual city that is involved eternally with the historical one.   (p. 214)

At this point Mrs Spark, typically, does not allow Barbara a blinding flash of revelation. Instead, she gives her scarlet fever, and from the sermon she gets merely 'the erroneous impression of a sanctimonious voice pounding upon her physical distress' (p. 217). The word 'erroneous' is, from Mrs Spark, a generous hint as to the importance of the sermon. In spite of the distractions — the angry custodians, Barbara's illness — the sermon none the less crystallises for the reader the issues that have previously been offered as Barbara's unresolved thoughts. Through faith, the disparate elements of Jerusalem can be united. Doubts should not be worrying, since they are the concomitant of faith; without them faith would be irrelevant.

Barbara has to hide until she has recovered from her fever. Suzi Ramdez, Abdul's sister, finds her a safe house, and to his amazement Freddy discovers that a spy-ring operates from the same place, headed by one of his colleagues. He intercepts a message, and eventually the spies are caught. He also sleeps with Suzi, which confirms his sense of adventure – so much so that he advises Barbara to continue her pilgrimage after her convalescence instead of sensibly going to the Embassy for help and protection. But, on his return to Israel, Freddy suffers from amnesia. His two days of adventure are forgotten until he receives the shocking news from Harrogate that his mother has been brutally murdered by her companion. This theme of violence and treachery between employers and their companions is one which interests Mrs Spark and it recurs in her novels. In *Memento Mori* Jean betrays Charmian. In *The Bachelors* Mrs Bowles and Carrie quarrel continually, sometimes lapsing into hair-pulling and fighting. Physical violence culminates in murder in *The Mandelbaum Gate*, and in *Not to Disturb* the servants acquiesce with their employers' murder and suicide. What comes over to the reader is the claustrophobic nature of these relationships, the reluctant, resented mutual dependence erupting every so often into violence as a means of venting frustration at their own impotence. The shock of his mother's death jolts Freddy's memory of his· lost days, and events return gradually to his mind. He suffers anguish for in effect ignoring his mother's final, anxious letter, but Mrs Spark makes it clear that tearing up his reply was a symbolic gesture signifying release from her overwhelming dominance. She is sacrificed, as it were, for Freddy's liberation and maturity. After he has destroyed the letters, he embarks with a light heart on his adventures in Jordan, and Mrs Spark makes it clear also that the long-term effects of his experiences are highly beneficial to Freddy:

> Looking back at the experience in later years Freddy was amazed. It had seemed to transfigure his life, without any disastrous change in the appearance of things; pleasantly and essentially he came to feel it had made a free man of him where before he had been the subdued, obedient servant of a mere disorderly sensation, that of impersonal guilt. (p. 148)

Months later, in Kensington, Freddy remembers a flirtatious conversation he had had with Suzi, and we are told,

> it was always unexpectedly, like a thief in the night, that the sweetest experiences of his madness returned; he was amazed at his irresponsibility for a space, then he marvelled that he could have

been so light-hearted, and sooner or later he was overwhelmed with an image, here and there, of beauty and delight, as in occasional memories of childhood. (p. 272)

Freddy's life is changed by the realisation of his capacity for love and adventure. From being 'luke-warm, neither cold nor hot', Freddy has the satisfaction of a man who, if only for two days, has realised his potential. And the image of Christ's second coming 'like a thief in the night', suggests that at some level this experience, however wild and unreal in retrospect, overwhelms the rest of his humdrum life.

Having allowed Barbara Vaughan to exercise an independent judgement, to act by her own interpretation of morality, Mrs Spark then proceeds to demonstrate God's encompassing power. By a divine irony, Barbara's marriage to Harry is given the blessing of the Catholic Church. An enemy produces a false certificate, stating that Harry was baptised a Catholic, believing that this will prevent him from gaining an annulment of his first marriage. But in fact it enables the annulment, since Harry's first wife was not a Catholic, so the Church does not recognise the marriage. That the certificate is false does not matter, provided both parties and the Church believe it to be true. Mrs Spark gleefully cites Isaac's blessing of Jacob, bestowed and irrevocable, even though the means of obtaining it were based on deception; 'God had not been to Eton' (p. 19). Like that of Caroline Rose, Barbara's freedom is enclosed within God's domain. She does not know, as the reader does, the full extent of the divine irony that enables her to achieve (unusually for a Sparkian heroine) both personal happiness and spiritual contentment.

Or so we are told. But, as I suggested in Chapter 1, the fulfilment experienced by Barbara is not totally convincing. It is not nearly so convincing, for example, as that granted to the Ramdez brother and sister in this novel, the Arab couple who radiate zest and vitality. Uncommitted to religion or cause, they are 'merged in a pact of personal anarchism' (p. 99), and curiously they are the beneficiaries of Mrs Spark's overflowing attention and love. I say 'curiously' because the argument of the novel is concerned with relating religious commitment to everyday life, and Suzi and Abdul, in joyous pursuit of self-interest and financial gain, appear to contradict such an aim. They both emanate the kind of happiness and exuberance that one might reasonably expect to be reserved for the virtuous heroine at moments of spiritual revelation: not simply a crude allocation of reward for virtue, but rather that Barbara, in order to make her gradual self-knowledge convincing to the reader, should be given the affirmative warmth of tone which Mrs Spark grants to the Arab brother and sister. Anarchy cannot finally be granted authorial approval in this novel, but in a way it is Mrs Spark's potential emotional salvation that she cannot disguise her enjoyment of it. This exuberance occasionally recurs in later novels, disturbing the fine moral poise of her narrative. In *The Mandelbaum Gate*, while not specifically endorsing their way of life, she makes the anarchists' activities seem at times more positive than Barbara's pilgrimage, and this upsets the balance of the novel. Thus the problem of unity occurs in the exposition of *The Mandelbaum Gate* as well as constituting its theme. Barbara, intelligent and possessing 'the beautiful and dangerous gift of faith' (p. 18), represents one aspect of Mrs Spark's creative imagination. Her imaginative capacity for fun, adventure, romance and rebellion remains segregated, however, and confined to the 'foreigners'. Of course, the heroine is carefully made to participate in each of these kinds of experience; we are told that she is sexy, she has a love-affair, goes on a dangerous pilgrimage, throws up her job, but the impression is that she seldom does these things wholeheartedly. There remains an emotional reservation which extends from Mrs Spark's psyche to Barbara, and thus to the novel overall.

Barbara's quest for freedom from the confines of religious and political structures is reflected in the form of *The Mandelbaum Gate*, which is much longer and closer to a 'loose baggy monster'[2] than any of the novels preceding it. It is as near to a 'humanist' novel as Mrs Spark ever gets, and in it she allows her characters more freedom of choice than usual. This in part accounts for its length: options are offered by the author and explored by the characters and there is a sense of genuine alternatives. In this novel, as in no other, coherence emerges through the way in which individuals struggle through experience to understanding, rather than on a structural, teleological level where the ending bestows coherence on preceding episodes. It is untidy and crowded in comparison with Mrs Spark's usual elegance, but it is full to bursting with evocative description – sights and sounds and smells and tastes – and with generous characterisation. This seems to me a notable step forward, a welcome loosening of her former tight control. In a review Angus Wilson remarks on this new departure: 'I am delighted at the change and I admire her courage in making it. . . . I have increasingly felt that her books were on the edge of becoming machine-made essays in sprightly Catholic paradox. Their sheer skill and concision were hampering her development.'[3]

It is certainly brave to abandon a format at which you excel, and Mrs Spark herself evidently felt the significance of such a move. In an interview before *The Mandelbaum Gate* was published she said, 'It's a very important book for me, much more concrete and solidly rooted in a very detailed setting.'[4] It was important because so much of herself was poured into the novel, and in publishing it she rendered herself vulnerable to criticism from admirers of her former economy. The reviews were, in fact, mixed, and Mrs Spark has not repeated the experiment. Five years later, in 1970, she expressed dissatisfaction with it: 'I don't like that book awfully much . . . it's out of proportion. In the beginning it's slow, and the end is very rapid, it races . . . I got bored, because it was too long, so I decided never again to write a long book, keep them very short.'[5] She follows this prescription for her next five novels, and the tentative development illustrated by *The Mandelbaum Gate* lies dormant. Mrs Spark goes on to capitalise on her strengths, to refine and purify her art.

The Mandelbaum Gate is the last novel in which Mrs Spark makes the serious treatment of Roman Catholicism her central theme. In her later work the material world becomes much more dominant, its atmosphere caught by utilising a salient aspect of it, such as the *dolce vita*, inflation or terrorism, as emblematic of people's moods or behaviour. The former all-encompassing divine power becomes the *deus absconditus* manifest in the harsh milieux of most of her subsequent novels. This shift of emphasis is, I think, due to both external and internal causes: that is to say, the changes in the Roman Catholic Church itself, and the idiosyncratic evolution of Muriel Spark's own personal faith. The reforms of the Second Vatican Council (1962–5), intent on 'modernising' the Catholic Church, were welcomed by many Catholics,[6] but others, including Evelyn Waugh, were deeply upset by them. For the Church to adapt itself to changing times seemed to him a total contradiction of its function as a bastion against mutability and moral fashions. He wrote despairingly, 'I hope I will never become an apostate',[7] and for Waugh even to contemplate a loss of faith shows how much affected he was by the reforms. Muriel Spark makes the Abbess of Crewe highly scornful of liturgical and other changes, but she herself has expressed unorthodox views about the structure of the Church of Rome. In an interview she talked about this to Alex Hamilton, who wrote in 1974, 'She is a Catholic *faute de mieux*. This Pope is a disaster, so was the last. The Curia is a disaster.

They have to exist, but they ought not to be in Rome. She likes the idea of several Popes. Three would be a nice number.'[8]

Her impatience with the trappings of ecclesiastical power is not surprising, since irritation with the Roman Catholic establishment permeates her novels. What is more surprising is the dramatic shift in her beliefs which she expressed as early as 1970, without it apparently affecting either her faith in God or her continuing membership of the Catholic Church. She said,

> I don't believe in good and evil so much any more. No one makes pacts with the Devil, as they did in the Middle Ages. Now, there is only absurdity and intelligence. I'm sure that whoever was responsible for that massacre in Bel Air had no sense of actually doing evil, but rather they were vindicating something which was precious to themselves. . . . If we are intelligent, we will call it absurd.[9]

This is a remarkable statement, but one she has reiterated. In her address to the American Academy of Arts and Letters in 1971 she said, 'we have come to a moment in history when we are surrounded on all sides and oppressed by the absurd'.[10] And in *The Hothouse by the East River*, published in 1973, a character says, 'There's only one area of conflict left and that's between absurdity and intelligence' (p. 74). To substitute 'intelligence and absurdity' for 'good and evil' seems a form of profanity coming from Mrs Spark. In this way she has changed her definition of 'absurd', which she has formerly used or demonstrated in a manner echoing Kierkegaard. This philosopher is mentioned with approval in one of her short stories[11] (we are also told that his works are read by the Abbess of Crewe), and Kierkegaard's definition of the absurd finds resonance throughout Mrs Spark's early work. In *Fear and Trembling* he differentiates between two allegorical figures, 'the Knight of Infinite Resignation' and 'the Knight of Faith'. The latter

> makes exactly the same movements as the other knight, infinitely renounces claim to the love which is the content of his life, he is reconciled in pain; but then occurs the prodigy, he makes still another movement more wonderful than all, for he says, 'I believe nevertheless that I shall get her, in virtue, that is, of the absurd, in virtue of the fact that with God all things are possible.' The absurd is not one of the factors which can be discriminated within the

proper compass of the understanding: it is not identical with the improbable, the unexpected, the unforeseen. At the moment when the knight made the act of resignation, he was convinced, humanly speaking, of the impossibility . . . the only thing that can save him is the absurd, and this he grasps by faith.[12]

'Absurd' actions in this sense are illustrated in incidents such as Elsie's unexpected evidence at Patrick Seton's trial and the forged baptismal certificate in *The Mandelbaum Gate*. These incidents bring about a turn of events totally unpredicted by the characters. The absurd, Mrs Spark implies, is God-given, beyond the range of human scheming and accountability.

After *The Mandelbaum Gate*, and as her novels become less to do with religion, Mrs Spark's use of the 'absurd' changes. It loses its Kierkegaardian connotations, and reverts to its ordinary meaning of 'ridiculous'. It is not used in the totally pessimistic sense of non-Christian existentialism, since in Mrs Spark's economy man's purposeless state always contains the potential for redemption and significant use. She does not subscribe to a view of an absurdist world, but she clearly thinks that human behaviour is absurd in comparison with a divine pattern, and she portrays it as such. The comparison becomes less and less obvious, however, in the course of her work, discernible only by perceptive reading of hints and clues: Sister Helena unserenely gripping the bars of her grille; the final paragraphs of *The Public Image* and *The Driver's Seat*; the title *Not to Disturb*; the satiric tone of *The Takeover* and *Territorial Rights*. In fact, her work almost ceases to be comparative at all, very nearly becoming a statement of absolute fact about a fallen and godless world.

One of the ways in which Mrs Spark makes this increasingly secular statement is by transferring her attention from God's patterning in the world to men's designs for one another. As an analogy, she concentrates reflexively on the formal design which constitutes a novel, her protagonists being aware of their roles as manipulators of characters and events, and the narrator commenting on the novel's structure. As I suggested in Chapter 1, the difficulty for the reader of these reflexive novellas is that their moral force is only as powerful as the analogy is clear. Mauriac, in his *Bloc-notes* of 1953, says that 'At my age, the conflict between the Christian and the novelist has moved on to another plane. . . . A feeling that art is literally an idol, that it has its martyrs and prophets, and that for many people it is a substitute for God.'[13] Mrs Spark's work indicates that she is not unaware of this conflict, and it is aesthetic rather than religious endeavours which occupy the protagonists of her middle novellas. Whereas Nicholas in *The Girls of Slender Means* becomes a priest and martyr for his religion, Frederick in *The Public Image* in effect parodies this by killing himself at a site of early Christian martyrdom for the sake of his artistic, but real-life, plot. In *The Driver's Seat* Lise's death is dictated, as she sees it, by the necessary ending of the novel, and accordingly she submits to its aesthetic demands. Lister, in *Not to Disturb*, sacrifices his employers' lives to the perfection of his narrative, and in *The Hothouse by the East River* the characters have not ceased their lifelong manipulation of one another, even though they are in purgatory. The Abbess of Crewe does not consider purgatory, having happily abandoned the aspiration to possess an immortal soul for the immortality of art. The implicit theme of all these novellas is the pernicious transference of the principles of art to real life, and the dehumanisation it entails. It is a sin all the more insidious in that it is not so obviously wrong as murder or theft or fornication are to a Catholic. But in a way it is more so, just as Selina's ruthless insistence on poise and equanimity (and its appalling consequences) seems a deadlier and more chilling sin than the seaman's sudden act of murder.

The moral ambiguity of these novellas is lessened slightly in Mrs Spark's two succeeding novels, *The Takeover* (1976) and *Territorial Rights* (1979). This is not because they revert to a serious religious thesis, but, being longer and crammed with action and characters, there is therefore, in the author's view, more absurdity to mock. The novels are a satiric inquiry into the nature of wealth and ownership. In a world without religous faith as a source of security, material goods may seem a measure of stability, but Mrs Spark sabotages that belief. Faith in the material is shown to be misplaced and possession itself a farce; territorial claims, whether related to real estate or sexual monopoly, are dramatically undermined. Both these novels are set in contemporary Italy, where the impression is given that the twentieth-century decline and fall is speeded-up and intensified; this acts as emblematic of Mrs Spark's view of the world at large.

The majority of Mrs Spark's novels have a hermetic quality, dealing with enclosed communities or groups of people bound together by common circumstances. Tensions and influences are usually generated within the groups, or as a reaction to a supernatural or sudden event. *The Takeover* is exceptional in that the characters are strongly under pressure from the economic and political changes in the wider world, and Mrs Spark lays unusual stress on the process of transition which takes her characters unawares:

> It was not in their minds at the time that this last quarter of the year they had entered, that of 1973, was in fact the beginning of something new in their world; a change in the meaning of property and money. . . . Such a mutation that what were assets were to be liabilities and no armed guards could be found and fed sufficient to guard those armed guards who failed to protect the properties they guarded. . . . (pp. 126–7)

She proceeds to show that the apparent solidarity of things is illusory in a way that illustrates the nature of wealth in a time of inflation. Antique furniture is quietly dissipated by copies being made, and the originals sold. Burglars instal burglar alarms, or, posing as art historians, are courteously given a guided tour of the house they intend to burgle. All robberies are spectacularly successful: the only time a burglar alarm works is when Maggie, the novel's heroine, tries to get into her own house at night, and she is then taken into custody until identified. This kind of paradox is enjoyed by Mrs Spark, who, having made Maggie one of the world's richest women, makes her cheques bounce as her fortune decreases through swindle. Even bricks and mortar are not as solid as they would appear: Maggie's new house at Nemi turns out to be *abusivo*; that is, built on land fraudulently acquired, and thus is deemed not to exist. We learn that the property laws are very complex, very Italian. A claim to Maggie's *abusivo* house 'depends . . . on whether the land they own is only the top-soil. In Italy, sometimes the sub-soil belongs to somebody else; it could belong to the Church or the State' (p. 191).

The *status quo* is further disrupted by the increasing swing to the Left in Italian politics. The Communists achieve prominence in the regional elections, and Maggie's husband is extremely worried by this:

> The Communists became 'They', the Italian '*Loro*'. Berto said '*Loro, loro, loro* ... They, they ... They will come and take away everything from you ... They will kill ... ti liquideranno ...', said Berto. 'They will take over ...' (pp. 201–2)

It is no accident, of course, that Mrs Spark has named Maggie's manservant 'Lauro'. He is indeed one of 'them', not necessarily a Communist, but a rapacious opportunist such as Berto fears, who exploits Maggie and her family in every way he can. And yet Maggie and Lauro are very much alike, and it is their unacknowledged recognition of this (plus, as always, financial inducement) which makes them curiously interdependent. Maggie needs Lauro, an arch-survivor, to help her to survive too, and she uses him intelligently. They are both immoral, but no such judgement is passed on them within the novel. Nor does *The Takeover*, despite the opportunities, at any point provide an explicit homily on the transience of worldly wealth. In fact, Mrs Spark makes the following observations on money, neutralising it from inevitably evil connotations:

> Indeed, money of any sort is, in reality, unspendable and unwasteable; it can only pass hands wisely or unwisely, or else by means of violence, and, colourless, odourless and tasteless, it is a token for the exchange of colours, smells and savours, for food and shelter and clothing and for representations of beauty, however beauty may be defined by the person who buys it. Only in appearances does money multiply itself; in reality it multiplies the human race, so that even money lavished on funerals is not wasted, neither directly nor indirectly, since it nourishes the undertaker's children's children as the body fertilizes the earth.   (p. 140)

The poetic style of that passage was formerly reserved by Mrs Spark for making deeply held religious statements, and its secular reuse, as it were, is symbolic of the distance Mrs Spark has travelled from her first novel. There is, however, a character in *The Takeover* called Pauline Thin, reminiscent of Caroline; that is to say, a young, strongminded woman of independent views, a Roman Catholic almost despite herself, and highly critical of some of her co-religionists. She shows no deference to two Jesuit priests who visit her employer, and this surprises them, although not us:

> 'I guess she isn't a Catholic,' said Gerald soothingly.
> 'I'm a Catholic,' said Pauline. 'But that's got nothing to do with it. One doesn't tell people all one's business and all one's employer's business.'   (p. 15)

Pauline's employer, Hubert, has founded a cult around the goddess

Diana, from whom he says he is descended. Secular forces in Mrs Spark's later novels often include what could be called religious substitutes – philosophic movements, psychoanalysts, dietary cults. In satirising them she draws attention not only to what she sees as their futility in comparison with Christianity, but also to the irony that it is a man's recognition of a spiritual need that gives rise to a series of secular cults to fulfil it. Pauline is not in the least taken in by Hubert's worship:

> 'To us,' said Hubert, 'who are descended from the ancient gods, your Christianity is simply a passing phase. To us, even the God of the Old Testament is a complete upstart and his Son was merely a popular divergence ...'
> 'Hubert,' said Pauline, 'you know I'm a Catholic. I don't mind helping you but you know I won't have my religion insulted.'
> (p. 107)

When Hubert holds a huge open-air meeting of his cult, Pauline attends, carrying a 'blackbound book'. 'Hubert thought it looked like his Bible but then he put the thought aside, not seeing what she could possibly want to do with it' (p. 219). Pauline reads a condemnation of the worship of Diana from the Acts of the Apostles and, with another English girl, disrupts the meeting. Hubert is very angry with her but, like Maggie, she is indestructible and tenaciously stays with Hubert, whom she loves. In the early Christian era the worship of Diana declined as Christianity gained strength, and the August festival of the goddess became transferred to the day of the Assumption of the Blessed Virgin Mary on 15 August. Both were addressed as 'Virgin Queen', and the subtle absorption of paganism into Christianity is paralleled in *The Takeover* by the Jesuits' recruitment of Hubert. Persuaded by Pauline, he is to run the Charismatic Movement in the Catholic Church (another satiric target for Mrs Spark), and is assured that 'it wouldn't be in conflict with Diana as the preserver of nature, not at all' (p. 261).

Although Pauline to some extent represents the resilience of the Catholic Church in a century that has reverted to paganism, her subsidiary role in *The Takeover* represents Mrs Spark's changing emphasis throughout her work. In *The Comforters* the Pauline figure is the central character, and her doubts and convictions about her faith are the main theme of the novel. In *The Takeover*, however, the central character is Maggie, and her methods of coping with inflation and lawlessness constitute the novel's principal concerns. Although we are assured of her indestructibility early in the novel, there is tension between the narratorial prophecy of survival and the calamitous events which surround her, and much of the suspense lies in wondering how she will cope with them. When she loses her money and her daughter-in-law's jewellery is thought to be stolen, Maggie outwardly panics:

> 'We're ruined!' Maggie shrieked back. 'We've all become paupers overnight, and the first thing that happens when a family is ruined is always a quarrel unless they are very rare people, very exceptional. . . . It isn't my fault if Mary's lost her jewellery. Maybe she hasn't. I hope not. I'm going to speak to Berto.' Maggie hung up at this point, looked at herself in the glass and was amazed to find herself still glowing and handsome.' (p. 241)

She is surprised to find that her power does not depend solely on her wealth, and swiftly adapts to the anarchy around her by adopting the same tactics: 'Why shouldn't I be a criminal? Everyone else is' (p. 246). Maggie survives, and the energy with which she goes about it echoes her literary predecessor, the Abbess of Crewe. Mrs Spark clearly likes Maggie; she is given narratorial approval for refusing to give in to worldly pressures, even though she counters them with similar immorality. There is no moral evaluation in this novel and, paradoxically, this omission makes an implicit moral point by giving the affairs of the world far less importance than is commonly attributed to them. If *The Takeover* is chronicling the decline of Western civilisation, it does so with a relaxed zest which at first seems inappropriate, then exhilarating. It suggests that nothing on earth is as important as we think and, having freed our minds from the fetters of this world, Mrs Spark sets us at liberty, if we so choose, to focus on the next.

Territorial Rights continues Mrs Spark's sharp, unsentimental scrutiny of contemporary problems, such as terrorism and political defection, which she leaves unobscured by emotional reaction. The effect is appalling, but it is also enlightening. We learn from *Territorial Rights* that some people have a vocation for evil, and that to pretend otherwise is to deceive ourselves. Set in Venice, the plot involves spies, adultery, murder, blackmail, betrayal, kidnapping and terrorism, plus, it is insinuated, any other sins you can think of which are not specifically mentioned. The complexity of the plot takes us a long way from the uncluttered story-line of Mrs Spark's elegant novellas. The 'thriller' plot of *Territorial Rights* is similar, in its self-conscious derivation, to the diamond-smuggling plot in *The Comforters*. But, whereas the 'obvious' plot in that novel concealed another (that of Caroline's involvement in the fiction-making process), there is no such reflexive sub-plot in *Territorial Rights*. The fictive-sounding plot, with all its clichés, is established as realism by Mrs Spark, who accepts and capitalises on its unrealistic aspects and its absurdities. No longer is the difference between appearance and reality made a moral issue as in *The Public Image*. It is as if Mrs Spark, after living for years through the dramas of contemporary Italy, has abandoned her belief in any such difference. *Territorial Rights*, in common with *The Takeover*, has an exuberant air of deliberate superficiality, a refusal, almost, to engage profoundly in moral issues when survival without hypocrisy is about the most one can hope to achieve. This is not the same as saying that Mrs Spark has surrendered to an absurdist attitude. It is tantamount, however, to saying that, like Evelyn Waugh, she has withdrawn to a high and distant viewing platform from which she chronicles the activities of the world as she sees them. Like Waugh's, hers is still a Christian perspective, which, paradoxically, saves her from pessimism, since it would be more disturbing to her if a godless world were virtuous. This accounts for her light-hearted approach, for her resolute seizing on what is funny or beautiful or ripe for satire.

In *Territorial Rights* Mrs Spark's satire is indiscriminate; no absurdity escapes her if she considers it worth deflating. Lina, a Bulgarian defector, is passionately anti-Semitic. After remarking casually that this lost her most of her friends, Mrs Spark, with narratorial mischief-making, has her sleep with a Jew. Lina jumps into a canal to purify herself from such contamination, and, Venetian canals being what they are, she has to be given antibiotics against infection. Similarly, Lina's artistic talent is mocked by the narrator when it is used for propaganda purposes: 'she went to the Black Sea and did work-groups at the docks all looking in the same direction, very tanned; and she excelled at women, large and strong, coming out of a shoe factory near her home, all looking healthy and refreshed after a good day's work' (p. 69). However, having ridiculed Lina's application of her talent, Muriel Spark then allows her to correct another character's superficial preconceptions of an artist: ' "You look every inch an artist", she said to Lina. "It isn't what you look, for an artist, it's what you do", said Lina' (p. 99). That is a very Sparkian remark, which restores the balance in Lina's favour.

In the same way, the reader is at first lured into making a disparaging judgement of Anthea Leaver, the deserted wife whose adulterous husband is enjoying himself in Venice with his mistress. Anthea sits dully at home in a Birmingham suburb; Mrs Spark does not bring her to life and of all the characters she is the most wooden and stereotyped. But for all that she has a point of view. Lina says to her husband Arnold, 'You know it is all right for you to enjoy your holiday without a wife, but Mrs Tiller should not have come with you. . . . I can also see the point of view of the good and faded wife' (p. 186). Having dismissed Mrs Leaver (with the connivance of Mrs Spark) the reader is now forced to re-evaluate her, to admit that her anxieties and actions have their due place in the narrative, and in themselves have some significance.

The theme of money pervades this novel, as it does *The Takeover*, although inflation is no longer stressed. The Bulgarians, Serge and Lina, are shocked at the Western attitude to money, and we are given a nasty description of Serge's London mistress, who hands out money to her children to get them out of the way. When Lina discovers a briefcase containing $150,000 (blackmail money, naturally), she returns it to its owner. Not that this represents a straightforwardly censorious attitude to wealth by Mrs Spark. Lina fears a trap, having learned to associate wealth with decadence. But although money is a dominant theme its effect is of a catalyst rather than a force for evil. The richest character, Curran, lives a life moulded by money and inseparable from it; Robert Leaver, the terrorist, comes to life earning his own living, as it were; Lina cannot cope with it; Mr B, the head of a detective agency, uses it as a weapon, insidiously: 'You're a very charming person, Mrs Leaver. I hope that money will not come into our relationship – at least, not to any appreciable extent' (p. 60). Grace Gregory and Mary Tiller have tremendous fun with it, enjoying travel and Venice and adventures to the full. This recent dwelling on wealth – its advantages and drawbacks – reminds us of Mrs Spark's knowledge and experience of the subject. We learn from *The Takeover* the problems of insuring jewellery of 'Maggie's sort' (p. 129) and from *Territorial Rights* the category of wealth currently considered worth blackmailing. 'Mary Tiller was not in the blackmail rich category' (p. 111), we are told. 'She won two hundred thousand in a lottery two years ago otherwise penniless' (p. 114).

Throughout her work Mrs Spark has had an affection for anarchic characters, which, with the exception of Dougal Douglas, have been included in the cast of the looser, less controlled and hence stylistically most appropriate novels. For example, there is Louisa Jepp in *The Comforters*, Abdul and Suzi Ramdez in *The Mandelbaum Gate*, and Maggie in *The Takeover*. Robert Leaver is their descendant in *Territorial Rights*, although his vocation is for evil, rather than for disinterested anarchic activity. Mrs Spark makes it clear that his alliance with his former kidnappers is the beginning of a personal fulfilment, previously equated in her novels with religious faith. As Robert walks into his hideout in the house of a blackmailer 'the thought came to him, with a rush of pleasure: At last I'm home – I'm out of the trap' (p. 221). We learn, furthermore, 'It was the beginning of Robert's happy days, the fine fruition of his youth' (p. 221). It is not pleasant to be told that terrorists are happy and fulfilled; we entertain pious hopes that they are bitter and vengeful, or tortured with guilt. Mrs Spark, however, is much more realistic about acknowledging the possibility of loving evil for its own sake:

'You're mistaken if you think wrong-doers are always unhappy', Grace said 'The really professional evil-doers love it. They're as happy as larks in the sky. . . . The unhappy ones are only the guilty amateurs and the neurotics ... The pros are in their element.'

(p. 235)

On reflection, this rings true, and yet another unpalatable realisation is forced upon us.

The activities of Mrs Spark's anarchic characters have become increasingly outrageous in the course of her work, so that Louisa's diamond-smuggling becomes, so to speak, the butchering of Pancev's corpse and Robert Leaver's murderous career. Mrs Spark's work, like that of Evelyn Waugh, presents us with the problem of how we react to shocking accounts of human behaviour. In her early novels these accounts were not so shocking, since Mrs Spark was then comparatively generous with her moral directives, and the reader was subtly assisted to read the text aright. In her later novels, however, the hints are all but omitted. In *Territorial Rights* Anthea complains about her husband leaving her, and says to a private detective, ' "Human nature is evil, isn't it?" His features did not change, nor his smiling lips open, but he made a small cynical snort. Then he said, "I wouldn't call it evil. Human nature is human nature as far as I'm concerned" ' (p. 60). The adjective 'cynical' distinguishes between the narratorial viewpoint and that of the detective, but it seems a meagre concession compared, for example, with Mrs Spark's near-satanic descriptions of Georgina Hogg and Patrick Seton. But as early as *The Ballad of Peckham Rye* Mrs Spark shows a tendency to present the reader with morally ambiguous texts, where her interest in amoral characters runs counter to her evaluation of their actions in terms of good and evil. By *Not to Disturb* the lack of explicit moral directives is such that the reader must take almost the entire text as a terrifying metaphor of contemporary society. *Territorial Rights* is another such metaphor. Mrs Spark cannot show God-fearing people if she believes they no longer exist, and in this novel she attacks both capitalist and communist ideologies, as if to indicate the futility of any godless creed. She is no longer a religious writer in the same sense as she was at the beginning of her work. But I would want to claim that she still writes *sub specie aeternitatis*, a viewpoint which enables her to communicate without panic or despair the various brief allegiances of the temporal world.

5 Plots and Plotters

The subject of plot-making fascinates Mrs Spark: both the fictional construction of a novel and the scheming activities of her characters. As a novelist who is also a Catholic, she is aware that her own fiction-making activities take place within what could be called 'God's plot', being a metaphor for the Christian belief in a divinely ordered universe. In her novels the stress is either on the plots laid by her characters, or reflexively on a demonstration of how plot functions in a novel. In each case she elicits our perception of a divine or a moral plot behind the obvious one, and the interest is heightened by the tension between the two, and how it is resolved.

In *The Comforters*, written shortly after her conversion, Mrs Spark subjects her protagonist to a sense of irksome constraint at being in a plot. Caroline struggles with the problem of exercising free will in a divine context, and her role as a Roman Catholic convert has frequent parallels with her role as a character in a novel. An audible, authorial voice exercises its omniscience over Caroline's actions, and she has to come to terms both with the voice and with the dictates of her faith. She says 'the fact of the author and the facts of the Faith . . . are all painful to me in different ways' (p. 107). She tries to assert her independence by attempting to outwit the voice's plans: 'I intend to stand aside and see if the novel has any real form apart from this artificial plot. I happen to be a Christian' (p. 117). She uses the fact of her Christianity – that is to say, her knowledge of her participation in a greater plot – to give her the confidence to stand aside from the ostensible plot and test its validity. But, as in Graham Greene's *The End of the Affair*, the narrator challenges God for the heroine, and involves Caroline in circumstances unforeseen by her. Gradually, she comes to realise that she has to reconcile her everyday life (the 'artificial plot' of the novel) with her new life as a Roman Catholic:

Her sense of being written into the novel was painful. Of her constant influence on its course she remained unaware and now she was impatient for the story to come to an end, knowing that the narrative could never become coherent to her until she was at last outside it, and at the same time consummately inside it. (p. 206)

In this way *The Comforters* argues the case for belief in a divine pattern for mankind. Mrs Spark suggests that understanding of our part in such a pattern is necessarily imperfect while we are participating in it. Only at the end of a life (when a person having been subject to its limitations finally transcends it) do events and people become significant, since a plot has emerged from their interaction, however imperfectly realised at the time. Caroline, through suffering, ultimately understands the Christian paradox that total freedom demands total submission to God's 'plot', which in turn brings understanding of its purpose. In *The End of the Affair* Graham Greene is more pessimistic than Muriel Spark, and allows only the saints to transcend the stratagem God creates for ordinary mortals:

> They stand outside the plot, unconditioned by it. But we have to be pushed around. We have the obstinacy of non-existence. We are inextricably bound to the plot, and wearily God forces us, here and there, according to his intention, characters without poetry, without free will, whose only importance is that somewhere, at some time, we help to furnish the scene in which a living character moves and speaks, providing perhaps the saints with the opportunities for *their* free will.[1]

Caroline has shared the pain of being 'inextricably bound', but her acceptance of it is a liberation. Her suffering – her voices and the everyday demands of her religion – combined with other people's lack of understanding, has given her an unpalatable insight. This is that the fact of her faith does not nullify the fact of evil, and this has to be accepted and made sense of through the gradual realisation that the commonplace and even the corrupt have an integral relationship with the extraordinary and the divine.

Mrs Spark makes Caroline Rose a writer who is working on a book called *Form in the Modern Novel* and, as it happens, is 'having difficulty with the chapter on realism' (p. 59), because, it is implied, she is becoming aware of realities which transcend phenomena. For similar reasons realism is not Mrs Spark's aim and her plots are elegant variations on one theme: she continually draws attention to the gap between this world and the next, and illustrates attempts to bridge it. In doing this, she is not afraid that the reader might doubt the autonomy of her fictional worlds; indeed, she courts that doubt by revealing the mechanics of her fiction-making, thereby alienating us from undue involvement in the plot. She does this because she wants our belief to go where her work points, and not to reside in her fictions. In *The Comforters* she demonstrates the fictiveness of one of her characters in a peculiarly surrealistic way. Helena says of Georgina Hogg, 'I am beginning to think that Georgina is not all there' (p. 175), and later she points out to Caroline that Mrs Hogg 'hasn't any life of her own' (p. 216). These everyday clichés are recycled by Mrs Spark to indicate Mrs Hogg's lack of a spiritual life, but they are also a joke about the fictional conventions taken for granted and used so conveniently by the realistic novelist. Having been introduced to characters in a novel, we usually assume their quiescent fictive existence somewhere in the background, even when one is not specifically mentioned. Mrs Spark, however, demonstrates through Mrs Hogg that fictional characters, constructs of the novelist, 'exist' only at the precise invocation of their creator. Thus Mrs Hogg is made to disappear – that is, attention is drawn to her disappearance – whenever she is not currently involved in the plot: 'as soon as Mrs Hogg stepped into her room, she disappeared, she simply disappeared. She had no private life whatsoever' (p. 177). A similar play on words is used in *The Hothouse by the East River*, where the main characters are, in fact, dead, and where the jokes about the artificiality of their life-style are simultaneously comments on their roles as characters in a novel. Pierre says contemptuously of his mother's friends, 'These people don't exist as far as I'm concerned' (p. 34). And when Katerina sees her mother blazing with jewels at a small off-off-Broadway theatre she asks, 'Am I on a trip or is she real?' (p. 106).

Such *double-entendres* are comparatively subtle reminders of the fictive nature of novels. Mrs Spark is deliberately far less subtle in revealing – or, rather, revelling in – the power of the omniscient narrator, who zooms in for a closer view of the characters and who spans years in a subordinate clause. *The Girls of Slender Means* has a particularly brisk narrator:

So much for the portrait of the martyr as a young man . . .

(p. 72)

We are in the summer of 1945 . . .   (p. 108)

The exposition of *The Takeover* is much more leisurely, but the narrator displays a similar lack of worry about being obvious:

But it is time, now, to take a closer look at Hubert. . . .   (p. 26)

Here are the details of the burglary:·. . .   (p. 128)

Anyway, back to Maggie's fortune:. . . .   (p. 140)

This sabotages our belief in the plots of Mrs Spark's novels because we are made highly aware that they are stories being told to us. She continues this process by making her plots derive from fictional stereotypes, such as the thriller, desert-island castaway tales, schoolgirl fiction, women's magazine romances, and the Gothic novel. *The Comforters*, for example, is almost a parody of a thriller-*cum*-detective-story, involving a diamond-smuggling gang, bigamy, blackmail, diabolism and . death. It is a conspicuously overdramatic plot, satirising expectations of such a 'low thing . . . as a novel' while simultaneously fulfilling them by exploiting such novelistic devices as coincidence and happy endings. *Robinson* clearly draws on the reader's preconceptions about castaways from *Robinson Crusoe* and *The Swiss Family Robinson,* and the tone and theme of *The Prime of Miss Jean Brodie* parody the conventional schoolgirl stories of Angela Brazil and Enid Blyton. *Not to Disturb* frequently reminds the reader of its debt to Jacobean tragedy and the Gothic novel. Fog rises from the lake and envelops the house. Wind howls round the shutters, lightning flashes, and a 'zestful cretin' raves in a locked attic: 'From an upper room comes a sound like a human bark followed by an owl-screech' (p. 53). This mixture of Mrs Radcliffe and the Brontë sisters, and the frequent dramatic and poetic allusions (which also occur in *The Abbess of Crewe*) confirm the novel as part of an established literary tradition. Mrs Spark does not seek to escape the connotations of such a tradition in order to claim originality. Rather she makes use of its implications to emphasise its inevitable relationship to former works of literature, and the acknowledgement of this debt further undermines the realism of a novel such as *Not to Disturb*, which reflects not real life, but methods of fictionalising it.

Non-literary preconceptions are also exploited to the full. The reader who associates religiosity with virtue is duly shocked by the behaviour of Mrs Spark's Catholic villains, and the impact of *The Abbess of Crewe* relies on our idea of a convent as a place of innocence and unworldliness. 'Foreigners' are also a useful source of prejudice – prejudice being a preconstructed mental plot which Mrs Spark economically seizes upon. For example, the sexual permutations in *Not to Disturb* and *The Takeover* are offered not so much realistically as to fulfil and simultaneously to mock our expectations about the way foreigners carry on; or, in *Territorial Rights*, to confirm suspicions that going abroad affects the British in peculiar ways. One of the English characters recounts by telephone her adventures to a friend in England: ' "It all sounds very far-fetched", said Anthea. "It may seem far-fetched to you, Anthea, but here everything is stark realism. This is Italy" ' (p. 161).

The fictional nature of Mrs Spark's plots is additionally emphasised by presenting them as ballads or fairy-stories. *The Ballad of Peckham Rye*, for example, is offered with a deceptive lightness, and with a succinctness influenced by the Scottish Border ballads. The events of the novel are given a distance, a fictionality, by passages at the beginning and the end, which firmly place the episodes of the novel in a distant realm of hearsay and fable. Near the beginning we are told, 'The affair is a legend referred to from time to time in the pubs when the conversation takes a matrimonial turn' (p. 12). And, at the end, 'Much could be told of Dougal's subsequent life. . . . for economy's sake, he gathered together the scrap ends of his profligate experiences – for he was a frugal man at heart – and turned them into a lot of cockeyed books' (pp. 200–1). The mock-deprecation of fiction at the end of this extract conveys Mrs Spark's awareness of its superficial untruthfulness, and a similar distancing process takes place in *The Girls of Slender Means*. The novel begins with the fairy-tale words 'Long ago', as if to announce its own legendary and allegoric quality. We are jolted, however, by the realism of the succeeding date – 'in 1945' – which is not swathed in the mists of time and which indeed is a date of historical precision and significance. The opening words, then, suggest the possible parabolic nature of the novel, within a realistic context. It ends with exactly the same words, but by then the distancing has taken on a touch of irony, since in the course of the book we become assured of the timelessness of its theme, which is the immanence of evil and its deceptive forms.

This somewhat contemptuous treatment of plots by Mrs Spark has the effect of denying them any originality at a purely narrative level. It is partly as if she makes a gesture deliberately hackneyed to show

how insufficient for her purpose is a mere 'story'. Thus, having established the story-line as less than fulfilling, she proceeds to what in her eyes are more important events, such as the analogy between the world and the book, and the revelation of apparent contingency as true design. This is particularly true of *The Driver's Seat*, which, besides being a macabre parody of a 'holiday romance' theme, becomes an open demonstration of the relationship in a novel between random events and their ultimate significance. By the end of this book the reader realises the inexorable connections between contingency and plot which are common to all novels (even those explicitly denying a coherent plot) but which are made obvious in *The Driver's Seat* because the author, having given away the ending with calculated panache, allows us to see the process of selection which leads to it. In an ordinary thriller, our understanding of the plot is retrospective, only the end revealing all the links in the chain. In *The Driver's Seat*, because the ending is known near the beginning of the novel, our understanding of the significance of minor events is progressive. This is a different, a more economic satisfaction: we see how the author creates a plot, while simultaneously enjoying the plot itself. Thus, as we learn that Lise is to be murdered, random statements take on additional meanings. For example, when she is told 'you and my nephew are meant for each other' (p. 103) that sentence can be variously understood. First, as a cliché redolent of a Barbara Cartland novel, which then becomes reinvigorated and made realistic by the speaker's conviction of its romantic appropriateness to Lise and her nephew. Secondly, the same sentence becomes ironic to the reader who realises that the heroine has already marked the nephew out not for her lover, but as her murderer. Lastly, the sentence carries the implication that the nephew is meant for Lise because the author has specially created him for her, that he is indeed 'meant' since he has been brought into existence to fulfil Lise's destiny as a character within a novel. Thus, *The Driver's Seat* exploits the conventions of a detective novel in order to reveal the mechanics of plot-making. Clues are carefully planted, coincidences arranged, irrelevancies and red-herrings coped with. Suspects are introduced and given alibis; motive and opportunity are arranged. For instance, Lise buys a dress, then angrily refuses it when the sales girl points out that it is stain-proof. Why does she need a dress that stains? Why does she buy such unforgettably vivid clothes? We are soon told why. She draws attention to herself so that witnesses will remember her, and buys a dress that will, of necessity, stain with her blood after the murder.

Throughout the narrative, Lise co-operates in the fulfilment of her plot, which, although imposed by the novelist, she takes over and makes her own. Lise, in the driver's seat both literally and metaphorically, relinquishes her grasp on the plot only after she is dead.

Besides revealing how a novelist constructs a plot, Mrs Spark's fiction contains a host of other manipulators: blackmailers, lawyers, film-directors, teachers, who may succumb to the temptation of imposing their plots on people in real life. Blackmailers recur. In *Robinson* we are told 'Life is based on blackmail' (p. 145) and this cynical view is frequently illustrated. Mrs Spark represents blackmailers as a force for evil, and, although they are not always punished within the novel's time-span, the implication is that they will encounter justice in the next world if not in this one. They are often made to seem physically disgusting, like Georgina Hogg in *The Comforters* or Billy O'Brien in *The Public Image*. Annabel's lawyer says of O'Brien, 'I was glad to have a shower after being in a taxi with him all the way from the airport' (p. 187). Patrick Seton, in *The Bachelors*, is one of Mrs Spark's most repellent creations. He is a medium, and an expert manipulator. It is no accident that Mrs Spark makes him guilty of 'fraudulent conversion', the *double-entendre* relating both to his financial and his spiritualist activities. Patrick plots the course of other people's lives in order to make them conform to his fantasy world, and he does not recognise or respect the given pattern of circumstances or coincidences ordained by his divine rival, which are to be his downfall. Ronald Bridges, whose profession of graphologist enables him to detect forgeries, seeks after the truth personally as well as professionally. In a small episode in *The Bachelors* he demonstrates his integrity by refusing to be blackmailed. He is anxious to retrieve a letter stolen from him by a lonely girl called Elsie, who, eager for his friendship, offers to return it if Ronald will spend the night with her. He refuses, so she lowers her terms: ' "If I give you the letter will you promise to come and talk to me again?" "No", Ronald said' (p. 183). He consistently refuses to implicate Elsie in a relationship based on her blackmail, and when eventually she returns the letter to him she has been given the freedom to make a selfless gesture, and she achieves a small measure of moral independence. Blackmail depends on secrecy, and its prevalence in Mrs Spark's novels reinforces the impression that she has a bleak view of human nature, with its sins and guilt and their lack of expiation, which create a climate ripe for exploitation. She implies that confession and absolution, even of a secular nature, would make the blackmailer redundant. Where blackmail is publicly exposed in her novels it entails a display of honesty and courage, such as that shown by Elsie at Patrick's trial, and by Annabel at Frederick's inquest. Tom Wells and Georgina Hogg are defeated in physical confrontations where the struggle is also symbolic of the battle between good and evil, and Wells's defeat is given a secular endorsement by a lengthy prison sentence some years later.

Mrs Spark's attitude to less mercenary manipulators is increasingly ambiguous. On one hand, their schemes are shown to be in opposition to God's 'plot'; on the other hand, Mrs Spark clearly recognises that their desire to control people and events is similar to that of a novelist, who shares a compulsion to influence by deception if only temporarily. As Angus Wilson puts it, 'Novels are lies, novelists disreputable people in their basic nature. . . . Gossip, confidence trickster, huckster, or novelist, all are kept in action by the power of narrating.'[2] Of course, novelists are licensed liars, and privileged in that they can exercise their fantasies and their power within an acceptable format, but Mrs Spark suggests that the habit, once formed for fictional purposes, is not easily broken. Charmian Colston, in *Memento Mori*, cannot restrict her imagination formerly used in her career as a writer, but imposes it on past events: 'her novelist's mind by sheer habit still gave to those disjointed happenings a shape' (p. 58). She treats real life as if it were one of her novels, selecting, arranging and editing material to suit her purpose. While recognising that 'the art of fiction is very like the practice of deception' (p. 210), she refuses to acknowledge that in real life too she has turned deception into a fine art.

The danger of this process is realised by Nicholas Farringdon in *The Girls of Slender Means*. He is aware that he is succumbing to the temptation of romanticising the girls at the May of Teck club, which he sees as an ideal society. The reader, through the practical eyes of Jane Wright, is shown, however, that Nicholas's views are not in the least shared by the girls themselves:

She did not see the May of Teck Club as a microcosmic ideal society; far from it. The beautiful heedless poverty of a Golden Age did not come into the shilling-meter life which any sane girl would regard only as a temporary one until better opportunities occurred.
(p. 80)

Nicholas, when he becomes aware of the fictionalising he is indulging in, 'discerned with irony the process of his own thoughts, how he was imposing upon this little society an image incomprehensible to itself' (p. 89). Paradoxically, Nicholas's acknowledgement that his image is a false one does not wholly negate it. We are not allowed to discount his vision of the club, since Mrs Spark insists on some kind of potential for it. We are told that 'it stirred his poetic sense to a point of exasperation' (p. 89), and the implications of communal poverty clearly conjure images for Mrs Spark's 'poetic sense' too. After assuring us of Nicholas's acceptance of the discrepancy between his viewpoint and that of the girls, his vision is then endorsed in a passage beginning with the words 'in fact', which in Mrs Spark's work always precede statements to be taken with the utmost seriousness:

> In fact, it was not an unjust notion, that it was a miniature expression of a free society, that it was a community held together by the graceful attributes of a common poverty. He observed that at no point did poverty arrest the vitality of its members but rather nourished it. Poverty differs vastly from want, he thought.
>
> (pp. 106–7)

The hostel may conform in part to Nicholas's plot, but its individual members do not. When he falls in love with Selina he tries passionately to endow her with all the qualities he desires to find in her. She seems to embody all the collective loveliness and grace he perceives in the May of Teck club, and he finds it hard to accept that her mind and her emotions are not as beautiful as her body:

> He wanted Selina to be an ideal society personified amongst her bones, he wanted her beautiful limbs to obey her mind and heart like intelligent men and women, and for these to possess the same grace and beauty as her body. Whereas Selina's desires were comparatively humble, she only wanted, at that particular moment, a packet of hair-grips which had just then disappeared from the shops for a few weeks. (p. 116)

Obsessed with what he wants her to be, Nicholas refuses to see Selina as she really is until the reality is too terrible to be ignored.

Selina is obviously a potent stimulus for a poetic imagination, but like Henry James Mrs Spark appreciates the strength to a writer of even a meagre stimulus: 'I don't think really, that in order to describe

somebody's life, you need more than just ... glance through an open
door as you're going upstairs, and catch a glimpse of the room before
the door shuts, and that's enough to elaborate on.'³ And in *Loitering
with Intent* Fleur for an artist says, 'I always preferred what I saw out
of the corners of my eyes, so to speak' (p. 38). In Mrs Spark's novels
her characters are frequently shown to be obsessed by a 'glimpse', or
teased by an image which leads them almost involuntarily to create a
plot to accommodate it. Lina Pancev, in *Territorial Rights*, is entranced
by a snatch of conversation she hears about a child walking to a
dancing class in Moscow, in 'her bronze velvet dress with lace collar
and cuffs' (p. 76). Her imagination works on the vignette,
romanticising Russia in her mind so that her idea of it is in
contradiction to the version of deprivation and hardship in fact being
related. In the same way she listens eagerly to her cousin Serge's
description of London, and he becomes, unwittingly, a manipulator of
the truth, and consequently, of Lina's life: 'He was unaware that the
same story that can repel can also enchant, according to the listener. It
happened that Lina's imagination was inflamed with the exciting
possibilities of western life, the more Serge reported what he had
perceived as hilarious decadence' (p. 74). A similar process is described
in 'The Go-Away Bird', where Daphne, confined in Africa, listens
avidly to an art-master talking disparagingly about England and its
treatment of artists: 'Daphne took home all such speeches of
discouragement, and pondered them with delight: "Soho", "poet",
"attic", "artist" ' (*Collected Stories I*, p. 326). Both Lina and Daphne
are disillusioned when they actually visit England, having
superimposed their own image of reality upon the versions told to
them.

A poetic image is one way of rearranging reality to suit one's vision
of it. In *Memento Mori* Mrs Spark shows us a scientific version of the
same process, which is practised by the amateur gerontologist Alec
Warner. Alec keeps an elaborate card-index on all his friends and
acquaintances over seventy years of age, noting methodically their
symptoms of physical and mental deterioration. His method is shown
to be an inadequate account of the events enclosed within Mrs Spark's
greater plot, since by refusing to acknowledge the spiritual aspects of
death he is distorting his subject-matter. Trial scenes in Mrs Spark's
novels have the same effect of distorting truth. In *The Bachelors* Ronald
Bridges realises that Patrick's trial has all the rituals and conventions
of fiction, the opposing counsels each trying to persuade the jury that
their version of the plot is the true one. And to achieve this the

characters involved take on specific roles (counsel, judge, jury, prisoner) and even use the deceptions of dressing up in costumes and adopting temporary attitudes for their performance: 'Ronald had put on his best dark suit for the occasion. . . . He had never before seen Martin Bowles in his wig and gown in court; it was an amazing sight. Martin had become instantly wise, unimpeachable' (p. 211). As Prosecuting Counsel, Martin seeks to prove that Patrick is guilty of fraudulent conversion, a sin (although carefully not a crime) Martin himself is committing on a much larger scale. Ronald is very aware of the irony involved, which is emphasised in the text by the juxtaposition of his thoughts with Martin's formal accusations:

'You admit', said Martin, 'that you accepted two thousand pounds from a woman of middle age?'
And you deny, thought Ronald, that you are swindling Isobel Billows? (p. 225)

'I suggest that your relations with Mrs Flower were of an intimate nature', said Martin.
'I deny it', said Patrick with an elaborate air of gallantry.
'And that you used these intimate relations to gain an influence over Mrs Flower?'
And, thought Ronald, on the strength of these intimate relations you obtained control of Isobel Billows' money. (pp. 225–6)

The Eichmann defence, too, described in *The Mandelbaum Gate*, offers an alternative plot to the truth of his wartime career, and the remote legal jargon distances the horror by restructuring it into a complex and meaningless pattern of words.

In her later novels Mrs Spark plunders the techniques of film and drama to construct her plots, and they reflect the immediacy and theatricality of those media. Not only do her characters display confident familiarity with the influential force of the visual image, but she herself works from the viewpoint of a film-director to convey atmosphere and mood. In *The Public Image* Annabel sees the streets of Rome as in a horrifying film:

The poisoner behind the black window-square, a man flattened against a wall with the daggers ready ... she wondered how the film would end, and although she wanted to leave the cinema and go home, she wanted first to see the end. . . . The camera swung round to the old ghetto. Fixed inventions of deeds not done, accusations, the determining blackening of character.   (pp. 92–3)

As with a film-director, a sense of image is part of Mrs Spark's creative equipment, but her use of it changes in the course of her work. In her early novels she dwells on outward forms before revealing them as emblematic. Later novels acknowledge, blandly and seemingly as a matter of contemporary fact, that image is all, that the superficial is also the essence. With scarcely perceptible irony at this state of affairs, Mrs Spark accepts that the novelist, digging deeply, is less likely to capture what now constitutes the truth than by skimming the surface, recording lightly the transience of instant fashions and behaviour. Indeed, the instantaneous image of the film appears more relevant and better suited to convey the present swiftly changing scene. Thus, while Annabel Christopher is eventually allowed to be able to distinguish between her self and her public image, Alexandra in *The Abbess of Crewe* conceives of no such distinction. Her style is herself; false, histrionic, unrealistic though it is. Alexandra, in common with other characters, such as Lise, Maggie and Robert Leaver, is not content to remain subject to the exigencies of narratorial plot, nor to the narrator's tendency to reveal discrepancies between image and reality. Instead they invent their own plots, using cinematic terms such as script and scenario, and marshal relevant facts and evidence to fit them. The Abbess of Crewe excels at this: ' "What are scenarios?" says Winifrede. "They are an art-form," says the Abbess of Crewe, "based on facts. . . . They need not be plausible, only hypnotic, like all good art" ' (p. 106). In *Territorial Rights* the blackmailers work from the fact of Victor Pancev's body, and invent a scenario around it. ' "Let's say Curran killed Pancev", said Robert' (p. 218). ' "Put in anything and everything," Giorgio advised, "and what you don't know, make up." Another time, Giorgio said, "What I'm telling you is true, or as near as . . ." ' (p. 221).

These scenarios may not be convincing in themselves, but they are certainly hypnotic in the context of the novels, and their imaginative creators are granted narratorial approval within the novels for their inventiveness. Indeed, in her later novels, it is as if Mrs Spark sees plots on a global scale and as much of a threat as those imposed by individuals upon one another. She seems prepared to back characters who attempt to resist their ingurgitation by the forces of twentieth-century society. Elsa, Alexandra, Maggie and Robert Leaver are allowed to flourish when they counter an absurd world with their own versions of reality. Maggie and Robert do not so much plot as adapt themselves to the times they live in, although in *Territorial Rights* Robert plans a gratuitous and shocking piece of nastiness. He lures Pancev's daughter, Lina, to dance unknowingly on her father's grave. We are given no motive for this, but presumably Robert is unable to resist the opportunity of bringing a cliché to life in such a startling fashion. (This macabre event is echoed in *Loitering with Intent*.) Often it seems indeed that the only admirable quality in Mrs Spark's later characters is their sheer refusal to succumb. Self-reflection and psychical immolation have become luxuries: in an inflationary world survivors have to take the place of martyrs.

The Abbess of Crewe is a survivor. The novel named after her was occasioned by the Watergate scandal surrounding Richard Nixon's second term as President of the United States; Mrs Spark pounced on the opportunity to transform this into a fiction at once satirical and speculative about power and its purposes and justifications. But, although there are parallels with Watergate of narrative and characterisation (particularly the Kissinger-like figure of globe-trotting Sister Gertrude), this novel lacks the didactic weight of satire. The effect of Alexandra is mesmeric rather than satiric. She outclasses Nixon at every point, and makes him look, in comparison, not evil, but merely amateur and inept. At one point Mrs Spark gives the Abbess an apparently heavy-handed joke about Watergate. Referring to the infamy of her convent she says, 'Such a scandal could never arise in the United States of America. They have a sense of proportion . . .' (p. 23). In the context of Alexandra's efficiency, however, this is not irony, but a criticism of Nixon's mismanagement. For those committed to evil, the Abbess later implies, a sense of proportion or limitation is a typically bourgeois handicap. We are told at the end of the novel that the Jesuit conspirators, presumably in an attempt to remedy this deficiency, 'have fled the country to America and are giving seminars respectively in ecclesiastical stage management and demonology' (p. 126).

Alexandra is determined to survive by turning himself into 'an object of art' (p. 125). Like Lise, she is obsessed with imposing a plot on random events; unlike Lise she has no fleeting regrets, nor does she have any remorse for the perversion of her religious vocation. 'To be the Abbess of Crewe is my destiny' (p. 39), she says, referring as much to the finished novel of the same title as to her forthcoming election. Appropriately, at the end of the novel she says in triumph, 'I am become an object of art, the end of which is to give pleasure' (p. 125). The novel does give pleasure, since a serious assessment of Alexandra's megalomania is not attempted, indeed is not admitted in any way by the narrator. And in the final paragraph, where a different perspective often appears or reasserts itself in Mrs Spark's novels, she is given an elaborate and sustaining endorsement, which implicitly grants approval to her activities throughout the novel.

In order to achieve her immortality, Alexandra sets herself up as a mythological figure, beyond human fallibility and outside the confines of history: 'modern times come into a historical context, and as far as I'm concerned history doesn't work. Here, in the Abbey of Crewe, we have discarded history. We have entered the sphere, dear Sisters, of mythology' (p. 20). Having elevated herself at the timelessness of myth, Alexandra revels in her god-like status. She is Jean Brodie intensified. Just as Miss Brodie exempted Rose from the common moral code, so Alexandra makes herself immune from moral responsibility and legal judgement:

> We are truly moving in a mythological context. We are the actors; the press and the public are the chorus. . . . As for the legal aspect, no judge in the kingdom would admit the case. . . . You cannot bring a charge against Agamemnon or subpoena Clytemnestra, can you?   (pp. 24–5)

The language of *The Abbess of Crewe* reflects Alexandra's ability to adapt rhetoric for use as a weapon. There is almost no gap between the viewpoint of the Abbess and that of the narrator; the reader and Alexandra's compliant nuns are mesmerised by the high-flown diction, the lavish quotations from English poetry, the Bible and Machiavelli, all of which Alexandra uses as she deems appropriate to obscure her real designs. This is made evident by the letter she composes to Rome to justify her peculiar activities in the convent. She asks her nuns, 'How does it strike you? Will it succeed in getting them muddled up for a while?' (p. 33). Later in the novel she fends off the press by giving them a quotation from Milton, saying happily, 'Garble is what we need, now, Sisters' (p. 103). Garble, of a high order, is what we get, and like the nuns the reader is amazed at Alexandra's style, amused at her jokes, and dazzled by her facility with words. When practical issues are raised, however, she is quite capable of dealing with them in plain language:

'. . . do you think the deserters can have discovered that the convent is bugged?' says Mildred.

'Not on your life', says Alexandra. 'The laboratory nuns are far too stupid to do anything but wire wires and screw screws. They have no idea at all what their work adds up to.' (p. 50)

This striking variation in register confirms the reader's suspicion that the Abbess uses language as a smoke-screen where necessary, and in assessing this novel it is tempting to extend this suspicion to her creator. As in *The Driver's Seat* and *Not to Disturb*, Mrs Spark adopts a tone which allows no room for reflection, and in *The Abbess of Crewe* there is no hint of narratorial pity for any of its characters, not even at the end of the novel. Although by any normal standards Alexandra is mad, it is quite impossible to feel sorry for her, since she is so indulgently treated by her narrator. Nor can we feel sympathy for Felicity, a nun who symbolises the liberal, reforming aspects of the Catholic Church, and who 'will never see the point of faith unless it visibly benefits mankind' (p. 43). Felicity, who by practising what she advocates, merely commits sins of the flesh, is far outclassed by the Abbess and her fellow-conspirators. 'The nasty little bitch can't stand our gentleness' (p. 74), they exult, and it is Felicity, vulgarly suffering from guilt, who ends up in the hands of a psychiatrist, an extreme punishment in Mrs Spark's canon.

In his review of this book, John Updike nailed its chief discrepancy: 'But, confusingly, although the author cannot approve of the Abbess Alexandra, she does love her, love her as she hasn't loved a character in a decade.'[4] I share the conviction of that 'cannot', and what is really being said is that Muriel Spark cannot be acknowledged as having written a purely frivolous novel. Nor has she: *The Abbess of Crewe* satirises power and its corrupting influence, the reforms of the Catholic Church, and the farcical nature of world politics. Clearly the reader is meant to discriminate between the internal logic of the convent and the moral standards from which it so flamboyantly departs, but the difficulty in doing so is the almost total identification of the narrator with Alexandra's viewpoint. In both *The Driver's Seat* and *Not to Disturb* the texts are dominated by obsessive viewpoints, but there are tiny clues that the narrator acknowledges 'another world than this'. There is no such acknowledgement in *The Abbess of Crewe*,

and, as with *The Takeover* and *Territorial Rights*, the reader must take
the entire novel as a shocking and disturbing metaphor.

The novels of Mrs Spark most explicitly concerned with plot and
counter-plots are *The Prime of Miss Jean Brodie* and *The Public Image*. I
want to look at these in some detail since they show both Mrs Spark's
knowledge and shrewdness about worldly methods of manipulation,
and her moral ambiguity towards her characters who are themselves
plotters and schemers. *The Prime of Miss Jean Brodie* shows an
individual planning other people's lives, and *The Public Image* turns
the image-making process into an industry. The religious perspective
of the former novel is changed in the latter, and Annabel's selfhood
becomes a moral rather than a religious issue. Both novels are analyses
of the temptation to play God in a world where his absence leaves a
dangerous void.

Jean Brodie is Mrs Spark's arch-manipulator. Her motivating
image is of her 'prime', and she is intoxicated by the power of her
own personality. As a teacher, she offers her own fictions for her
pupils' guidance. She quotes to them from the Bible – 'where there is
no vision the people perish' (p. 4) – but makes sure that the vision they
see is of her own ordering, which means that it is not, in her case,
divinely inspired. She is nothing so crude, however, as an unbeliever.
She goes to different denominations in rota every Sunday (excluding
the Roman Catholic Church – 'only people who did not want to think
for themselves were Roman Catholics' – p. 112) and 'She was not in
any doubt, she let everyone know she was in no doubt, that God was
on her side whatever her course' (p. 113). Mrs Spark has doubts,
however, and the theme of *The Prime of Miss Jean Brodie* is the True
Faith versus Miss Brodie's fictions. Like Patrick Seton she has a
Messianic complex. Patrick justifies his decision to commit murder by
equating his role with that of God: 'To make Alice into something
spiritual. It was godlike, to conquer that body, to return it to the earth
. . .' (p. 238). Sometimes in Mrs Spark's novels characters have god-
like qualities thrust upon them, and their rejection signifies their own
awareness of the right order of things. In *Memento Mori* a retired
policeman, asked to identify the mysterious telephone voice, says
wearily, 'The trouble with these people . . . they think that the CID
are God, understanding all mysteries and all knowledge. Whereas we
are only policemen' (p. 169).

Jean Brodie is convinced of the rightness of her own power, and uses it in a frightening manner: 'Give me a girl at an impressionable age, and she is mine for life' (p. 150). This is Miss Brodie's adoption of the Jesuit formula, but, whereas they claim the child for God, she moulds the child for her own ends. 'You are mine,' she says, '. . . of my stamp and cut . . .' (p. 129). When Sandy, her most perceptive pupil, sees the 'Brodie set' 'as a body with Miss Brodie for the head' (p. 36), there is, as David Lodge points out,[5] a biblical parallel with the Church as the body of Christ. God is Miss Brodie's rival, and this is demonstrated in a literal way when one of her girls, Eunice, grows religious and is preparing herself for confirmation. She becomes increasingly independent of Miss Brodie's influence and decides to go on the Modern side in the Senior school although Jean Brodie makes clear her own preference for the Classical. Eunice refuses to continue her role as the group's jester, or to go with them to the ballet. Cunningly, her teacher tries to regain control by playing on her religious convictions:

All that term she tried to inspire Eunice to become at least a pioneer missionary in some deadly and dangerous zone of the earth, for it was intolerable to Miss Brodie that any of her girls should grow up not largely dedicated to some vocation. 'You will end up as a Girl Guide leader in a suburb like Corstorphine', she said warningly to Eunice, who was in fact secretly attracted to this idea and who lived in Corstorphine. (p. 81)

Miss Brodie has different plans for Rose; she is to be a 'great lover' (p. 146), and her teacher audaciously absolves her from the sins this will entail: 'she is above the common moral code, it does not apply to her' (p. 146). This dismissal of possible retribution distorts the girls' judgement of Miss Brodie's actions. Her 'excessive lack of guilt' (p. 113) allows her to reconcile her Sunday worship and her affair with Mr Lowther, the music master, and this amorality infects the girls.

they in some way partook of the general absolution she had assumed to herself, and it was only in retrospect that they could see Miss Brodie's affair with Mr Lowther for what it was, that is to say, in a factual light. All the time they were under her influence she and her actions were outside the context of right and wrong. (p. 113)

Rose's destiny is designed primarily to fulfil, by proxy, Miss Brodie's passion for Teddy Lloyd, the art master. She renounces him because he is married, at the same time preparing Rose to take her place as his mistress. Rose and the other girls model for him, but such is Miss Brodie's influence over both the girls and the art master that the finished portraits invariably resemble Miss Brodie. This uncanny and rather sinister coincidence is emphasised by the fact that no other portraits in the studio look like Miss Brodie, only those painted of her girls. A perverse travesty of God, the girls are made in her image, a fact which delights her when she hears about it: 'Sandy . . . told Miss Brodie how peculiarly all his portraits reflected her. She had said so again and again, for Miss Brodie loved to hear it' (p. 160).

Sandy is Miss Brodie's principal confidante, and it is she who realises the extent of her megalomania: 'She thinks she is Providence, thought Sandy, she thinks she is the God of Calvin, she sees the beginning and the end' (p. 161). When Sandy discovers that Jean Brodie has precipitated the death of a girl by encouraging her to fight in the Spanish Civil War she realises that she will stop at nothing to fulfil her own desire for power. She informs the headmistress that Miss Brodie is a 'born Fascist' (p. 167), although this, as Sandy says later, is 'only a side line . . . but it served as an excuse' (p. 162). Sandy's abhorrence of Miss Brodie is not simply for her sexual or political intrigues, but for what they represent. This is her usurpation of God's role in the world, and her arrangement of other people's destinies.

Nevertheless, Sandy's betrayal of her teacher is complicated by the ambiguity of her motives, which are not necessarily as disinterested as they appear. Sandy herself is a plotter, and is fascinated by Miss Brodie's 'method of making patterns with facts' (p. 94). It is through Sandy's sharp little eyes that the reader observes most of the action of the novel. In particular, it is Sandy's viewpoint of Miss Brodie that predominates, and in her eyes that Miss Brodie finally stands condemned. The moral sophistication of Mrs Spark, however, is such that she denies us an endorsement of Sandy's condemnation. Miss Brodie's fate is engineered by her pupil, thus reflecting the very sin of which Miss Brodie is accused. But, apart from the fact of this 'coincidence', we are given no independent narratorial judgement on it, nor are we given Miss Brodie's interior thoughts and feelings, except as actually expressed to her 'set'. The reader thus has to rely on Sandy for her version of events, but there are doubts as to whether she is totally reliable as a narratorial guide, since she is more strongly influenced by Miss Brodie than she admits. As children, Sandy and Jenny write a series of imaginary letters between Miss Brodie and her lover, which they abandon as fantasy as they grow up. Sandy is shocked when she perceives that Miss Brodie's plans for Rose to sleep with the art master are not fantasy, but are in earnest: 'All at once Sandy realised that this was not all theory and a kind of Brodie game ... Miss Brodie meant it' (p. 159). She sleeps with Teddy Lloyd herself, not so much of her own volition, as to thwart Miss Brodie's plans. But there is a hint that she is jealous of his obsession with Jean Brodie; although he sleeps with Sandy, his portraits of her still turn out to look like her teacher. Our suspicions of Sandy's motives are reinforced by the strange description of her as a nun, later in life. She is not serene and composed, as after a right and justifiable action. Her betrayal of Miss Brodie has not brought her peace of mind, and her obvious agitation rather undermines our conviction in her judgement. 'She clutched the bars of the grille as if she wanted to escape from the dim parlour beyond, for she was not composed like the other nuns who sat, when they received their rare visitors, well back in the darkness with folded hands' (p. 43). At the end of the novel this is repeated, even more emphatically: 'Sandy clutched the bars of her grille more desperately than ever' (p. 171).

We are left uneasy. Mrs Spark, having provoked our righteous indignation at Miss Brodie's behaviour, proceeds to unsettle a little our moral composure. She reveals further refinements of ethical evaluation, by making us aware that Sandy is potentially as manipulative as Jean Brodie, as fond of plots, and that there are areas of judgement which are the disposition of God rather than man. As Lodge suggests,[6] she also gives us evidence to lessen the simplistic evaluation of Miss Brodie as 'evil' and Sandy as 'good'. When Sandy joins the Roman Catholic Church, we are told that she finds in its ranks 'quite a number of Fascists much less agreeable than Miss Brodie' (p. 168). In middle age Sandy at last realises that 'Miss Brodie's defective sense of self-criticism had not been without its beneficent and enlarging effects; by which time Sandy had already betrayed Miss Brodie and Miss Brodie was laid in her grave' (p. 114). The implication of that final clause is, 'By that time it was too late for Sandy to make amends', and there is here a belated realisation by Sandy that her judgement may have been at fault. This is not to deny Miss Brodie's megalomania, but rather to suggest that Mrs Spark's attitude to her is not as unambiguous as it first appears, and that there is implied in this novel a reluctant, conspiratorial admiration for her manipulative powers.

Sandy deliberately betrays Miss Brodie, and the theme of treachery threads through Muriel Spark's work. As in the novels of Graham Greene, Judas-like characters recur, and it is interesting that, like Greene, Mrs Spark does not automatically condemn her betrayers. Both, indeed, are ambivalent about the concept of loyalty. Graham Greene has said, 'I think loyalty to individuals, to people, means a lot to me. I don't feel a strong necessity for loyalty to an organisation, a faith or a country.'[7] Writing about the role of the novelist, he puts this even more strongly:

> I would emphasize once again the importance, the virtue of disloyalty ... Loyalty confines us to accepted opinions: loyalty forbids us to comprehend sympathetically our dissident fellows; but disloyalty encourages us to roam experimentally through any human mind, it gives to the novelist the extra dimension of sympathy.[8]

In an interview with Muriel Spark, Alex Hamilton writes that

> She herself is against family loyalties being imposed, or friendship loyalties. She feels very strongly about this. It's demanding too much of any human to ask them to be loyal to a party, to a system or a person for the whole of their life. To say 'You owe me loyalty' is a terrible thing.[9]

Sandy explains to Monica, another of Miss Brodie's girls, that ' "It's only possible to betray where loyalty is due . . ." "Well, wasn't it due to Miss Brodie?" "Only up to a point" ' (p. 170).

The point in Mrs Spark's novels usually occurs when the interests of an individual come into conflict with what she sees as higher interests, either religious or moral. This is not invariably true, however, since the motives for her betrayals can be selfish, altruistic or disinterested. In *Memento Mori* Jean Taylor says firmly, 'There is a time for loyalty and a time when loyalty comes to an end' (p. 191), and betrays the secrets of Charmian, her former employer, thus freeing Charmian's husband from a crippling burden of guilt and the threat of blackmail from other sources. But again, as with Sandy, we realise that Jean Taylor's motives may be mixed. Alec Warner asks, ' "Were you ever jealous of Charmian?" . . . "Of course I was," she said, "from time to time" ' (p. 191). In *The Girls of Slender Means* Jane is 'struck by a sense of her treachery' (p. 128) to her employer but also exhilarated by it. This is true also of Rudi, the German defector in *The Hothouse by the East River*, who envisages his fate as a traitor to his country, and talks to Elsa about it:

> he waves his hands towards the thick woods to their left and tells her that Hitler's parachutists will soon be filling these woods. He speaks with a sort of bitter, convinced pride like a Judas foretelling hellfires awaiting him as a boastful proof of his betrayed master's divinity. (pp. 64–5)

In the same novel Helmut Kiel is a suspected double-agent, and there is a further suspicion that he is gaining information about British intelligence from Elsa, who is sleeping with him. English spies recur in *The Mandelbaum Gate*, a novel humming with intrigue between Israel and the Arab world. But Mrs Spark sees treachery everywhere, not only between countries at war, but also between individuals who renege on their commitments to one another, or to God. It is a somewhat cynical view of human nature, summed up by Mrs Spark as 'a lack of expectancy',[10] and it is a view which pervades her work.

The theme of plots and counter-plots is expanded in *The Public Image*. Here we are shown image-making both on a professional and on a private scale: the manufacture of a film-star by the publicity industry, and the subsequent fictions invented by Frederick and Annabel. The novel is set in Italy, and, in common with the film industry, Mrs Spark capitalises on the theme of the Italian love of drama and sensational journalism. 'It's what they want to believe that counts' (p. 126) we are told, and Annabel Christopher's 'public image' is carefully tailored by a shrewd press-secretary to suit the demands of her audience. Although Annabel is a 'puny little thing' (p. 10) off screen, by some extraordinary photogenic quality she is transformed on it. She becomes known as the English Lady-Tiger, and this unlikely paradox is reinforced by the publicity about her marriage. Although she and Frederick are unhappy and frequently about to separate, they have a baby and are portrayed as an ideal couple: sophisticated and formal by day, their phlegmatic English appearance concealing a life of passionate sexuality by night. This image travels far and wide, even to England.

It was somehow felt that the typical Englishman, such as Frederick
Christopher was, had always really concealed a foundry of
smouldering sex beneath all that expressionless reserve ... Later,
even some English came to believe it, and certain English wives
began to romp in bed far beyond the call of their husbands, or the
capacities of their years, or any of the realities of the situation.

(p. 43)

In order to distinguish for the reader 'the realities of the situation'
concerning Annabel, the narrator reveals them in statements prefaced
by the words 'in fact', or they are given veracity by the use of the
words 'real' or 'reality'. For example, Annabel says, in contradiction
of her public image as a sex symbol, 'But in fact, in fact, I don't like
tiger-sex. I like to have my sexual life under the bedclothes, in the
dark, on a Saturday night. With my night-dress on' (p. 154). And we
are told, in the authoritative prose Mrs Spark uses to convey
certainties, that 'The baby, Carl, was the only reality of her life. His
existence gave her a sense of being permanently secured to the world
which she had not experienced since her own childhood had passed'
(p. 53).

The scenes of Annabel looking after her baby are tender and
practical, and depict one of the few genuinely loving relationships in
Mrs Spark's novels. It is as if Annabel's salvation, her outlet for true
feeling, is, temporarily, her author's also; the baby as a subject
providing an opportunity for the expression of warmth that, until
Loitering with Intent, Mrs Spark seemed unable to give to adult
relationships in her novels. When she is working Annabel telephones
the baby's nurse every three hours to see if he is all right, and she
refuses to allow Carl to become part of her publicity. Frederick
remarks unkindly on the suitability of the baby to Annabel's public
image as a devoted wife and mother, and the narrator comments, 'But
it was not that the baby fitted the public image, it was rather that the
image served the child so well' (p. 48). Thus, throughout the novel,
the baby acts as a moral positive, representing Annabel's reality, and
offering her an alternative way of life.

Frederick is jealous of the baby, a fact which, when he learns it,
shocks an Italian film-director so much that he 'was silent and forgot
for a while to be a filmman' (p. 147). Frederick is also jealous of
Annabel's success, and he too is caught up in the publicity
surrounding his wife and his marriage. His role-playing, however,

extends more deeply into his personality, since he has no professional
capacity in which to exercise it. Gradually we realise that it is
Frederick rather than Annabel who is increasingly unable to separate
fiction from reality. We are told that he 'hardly knew what was going
on' (p. 38), whereas 'Annabel was entirely aware of the image-
making process in every phase' (p. 41). Frederick cultivates 'a private
self-image of seriousness' (p. 33) and begins to criticise his wife's
acting on the grounds that she does not thoroughly feel, 'from the soul
outward' (p. 25), the parts she plays on the screen. Perversely, he
thinks she should experience as real what she is aware of as mere
acting. Annabel, however, has the integrity to make the distinction.
She applies skills and techniques to what she recognises as a job, and is
not squeamish about achieving the effect of sincerity through
professional skills. Frederick, on the other hand, begins to apply the
techniques of fiction to real life. Having lived in a world of scenarios
and watched the re-creation of his wife by professionals, Frederick
has learnt about plots – their design, execution and reverberations. He
formulates a real-life plot to rival that created by the film industry,
designed to smash Annabel's career. He commits suicide, having first
arranged a disreputable party at his wife's flat to coincide with the
time of his death. He leaves dramatic farewell notes (including one to
his long-dead mother), inventing and condemning Annabel's
appalling unfaithfulness, and destroying her public image of grace and
virtue. But Annabel, like Sandy, retaliates, and proceeds to thwart
Frederick's scenario. For all her warmth as a mother, Annabel is none
the less a very Sparkian woman; using all her skill as an actress and a
creator of fictions, she briskly and efficiently reorganises events in her
favour. After identifying Frederick's body in the middle of the night,
she returns to her flat to play the part of beautiful, young newly
bereaved widow: 'Annabel said to the doctor in audible Italian, "I
want my neighbours to come up to my flat with me. Everyone wants
their neighbours at a time like this" ' (p. 96). Seeing an American
reporter in the crowd she repeats this in English for the benefit of his
readers. Inside her flat her carefully achieved image is seriously
threatened by the voice of the doctor's child, blunt in its questions:
'why did he commit suicide and make a scandal for you?' Annabel
responds to this by using her own child to maintain her image, an
indication of her desperation, since she has previously been meticulous
in keeping the baby away from the media, because he has hitherto
represented her private, uncontaminated reality. In a calculated,
secular imitation of the sacrament of Communion she renews her

'spirituality' in the sight of her public, and acts out her role with cunning:

> Annabel started to weep over the baby, holding the glass awkwardly while she cradled the baby in one arm and secured him with the other elbow. She craned forward her head to sip the wine over the baby's body. The doctor put the aspirins half by half into her mouth and she washed them down with the warm wine and let her tears splash on to the side of the glass. (p. 101)

But the child's voice persists: 'The actresses can make themselves cry, they have to learn how to do it' (p. 101). The child is hushed, and, when the press arrive, Annabel and her neighbours are arranged and composed, 'as if the scene had been studied and rehearsed for weeks' (p. 105). She tells the journalists that Frederick's death was an accident, denies the party at her flat, and gradually reshapes the story. The morning papers, consequently, are in her favour, but her image is again threatened by the discovery of a comatose girl in her flat, who is taken to hospital suffering from an overdose of drugs after the infamous party. This does not fluster Annabel, who, like a resourceful novelist (and like her successors Lise and Lister), turns the unfortunate girl from a contingent into a significant character. Annabel makes her into one of the several women allegedly in love with Frederick, who hounded him to his death. She also becomes a focal point for Annabel's public forgiveness, a quality which the reader has already been told goes down well in the Italian press, being 'the only virtue which was exploited' (p. 37). Annabel plots thoroughly:

> Get Francesca to arrange my visit to the hospital this afternoon. I would like a bunch of yellow roses that look as if they've come out of someone's garden, newly picked – not all got up by a florist. Not too big, so that I can carry them easily. (p. 153).

On her arrival at the hospital, Annabel plays expertly to the crowd. She

> did not forget to look up at the hospital windows; sure enough, most of them were occupied by peering and bobbing heads. She placed her sad smile up there, too. . . . 'I am going to visit poor Danya,' she said, 'because I forgive her. . . .' (pp. 159–60).

Gradually, Annabel's plot replaces Frederick's, neither of which is the truth, because the truth is too mundane, too ambiguous and fragmented to make a coherent and believable story.

Near the beginning of the novel we are told that Annabel realises she will one day have to change or abandon her public image, but she experiences an Augustinian reluctance to do this: 'Not yet, she thought; not yet' (p. 49). When Billy O'Brien obtains Frederick's suicide notes, and blackmails her, the problem of maintaining her image is accentuated. Her lawyer arranges payment for O'Brien to suppress the letters, and with Luigi, her film-director, Annabel rehearses her role at Frederick's inquest. When it comes to the point, however, she has a change of heart. She produces the letters from her handbag, simultaneously destroying her public image for good. Afterwards her lawyer asks her why she did it, and she replies, 'I want to be free like my baby' (p. 190). She flies, unnoticed, to Greece, taking her baby with her.

In *The Public Image* there is a potent moral force which is not, as in most earlier novels, formalised into a specific religious faith. And unlike *The Prime of Miss Jean Brodie* this novel contains no suggestion that those who manipulate other people's lives are sacrilegiously usurping God's power. The struggle is between truth and falsehood, but on a secular level, so that our conviction in the story does not depend on our believing that Annabel chooses God rather than the devil, although the analogy is implied. When she learns that Frederick commits suicide by throwing himself into some deep excavations, the narrator ambiguously has Annabel think of 'that profound pit' (p. 86). Later she talks of 'all this hell in his death' (p. 148), but again the statement is left ambiguous, so that the equation of deception with the devil and the truth with God is not openly stated. Frederick chooses to kill himself at a place of former martyrdom. Ironically, a plot superior to his turns him, unwittingly, into a martyr to the truth, since his death enables Annabel to free herself from a life of deception. The film industry, Frederick, Annabel and Billy O'Brien all invent their separate plots in this novel; finally, none of them persists. What predominates is Annabel's reliance on her feelings for her baby. She is not aware of making a moral decision, but an instinctive decision, which in the context of the novel is shown to be morally right. The spare, cool tone of *The Public Image*, and its total lack of sentimentality, disguise the fact that it is unique amongst Mrs Spark's novels in its strong endorsement of instinctive action not finally contained within a religious framework. And it is typical of Mrs

Spark's reticence that she does not state outright the momentous nature of Annabel's decision to emphasise its importance and rarity within her novels as a whole. Instead, she ends *The Public Image* with a lyrical and moving passage:

> she felt as if she was still, curiously, pregnant with the baby, but not pregnant in fact. She was as pale as a shell. She did not wear her dark glasses. Nobody recognized her as she stood, having moved the baby to rest on her hip, conscious also of the baby in a sense weightlessly and perpetually within her, as an empty shell contains, by its very structure, the echo and harking image of former and former seas.[11] (p. 192)

This contrasts with Frederick's description of Annabel in his suicide note to her. He writes, 'You are a beautiful shell, like something washed up on the sea-shore, a collector's item, perfectly formed, a pearly shell − but empty, devoid of the life it once held' (p. 141). Unlike Frederick, the narrator at the end of the novel endows Annabel with a sense of belonging in the scheme of things. The image of empty, hollow beauty is revitalised. Both literally and symbolically Annabel has removed her dark glasses; without them she no longer projects the image of a film-star, but she sees clearly. She feels the baby is an intrinsic part of her, representing for her the potential of a new life, just as the sound of the sea in a seashell represents not hollowness, but the resonance of an inner wealth.

In all her novels Mrs Spark uses the theme of the plotter and fiction-maker to point out the prevalence of deceptions, and the danger when these people take it upon themselves to extend their fictions into reality. They hold and manipulate the strings, as it were, but almost invariably a sudden, unexpected action upsets the puppet-show. This disruption (the fire at the hostel, the unexpected evidence at Patrick's trial) changes what had seemed a predictable narrative sequence, or calls attention to its significant relationship with a divine or a moral plot, which has been immanent, but hidden, from the beginning. In Mrs Spark's early novels the narrative set up by the plotters is frustrated by divine intervention in the form of the supernatural. Later plots are disturbed by moral action effected through an individual's insight or decision, God's power at one remove. What the novels have in common, up to *The Driver's Seat*, is that the surface narrative is never allowed to run its course. But in *The Driver's Seat*, and in later novels up to *Loitering with Intent*, there is a further change in technique; the plotters are allowed to achieve their own ends. Lise, in *The Driver's Seat*, is an active, co-operative participant in the fulfilment of her destiny, which is her destruction. She tries to take over the plot-making, to become one with the creator of the story. Seeking her death, she fuses it with the end of the novel, and turns her fate into plot. The vehicle for her aspirations is the narrative, and she takes over the driver's seat figuratively by assuming control of the narrative (written in the present tense for the most part, since she constructs the story as it happens) and realistically in that she drives herself to her final destination where she plans to be killed. Luring a mentally ill man to kill her provokes no narratorial condemnation; indeed, there is almost admiration implied in the description of the elaborate procedure Lise undertakes to ensure her technical blamelessness. For a Christian, suicide is a sin, and by arranging to be killed by someone else, as Malcolm Bradbury points out, Lise makes 'theologically artful use of her own mortality. Lise has a soul to consider, and she makes the subtlest use of it she can, the most dangerous flirtation with suicide she might; she has all the casuistry of the higher Sparkian heroine, and in this partakes of her narrator to high degree.'[12] The theological implications of suicide are dwelt on by Graham Greene in *The Heart of the Matter*, and a comparison with *The Driver's Seat* shows how differently Muriel Spark deals with the same subject. Mrs Spark's protagonist is Jesuitical in her moral sophistication and she avoids the sin to which, with what appear to be the highest motives, Scobie succumbs. (In *Loitering with Intent* the narrator says 'I have always been impressed by Jesuitical casuistry' – p. 50.) Lise's action – or, rather, inaction – is chilling and rather shocking, contributing to what Bradbury calls 'an appalling *moral* manner, a splendid impudence'[13] which characterises Mrs Spark's later work.

Annabel's triumph is that she is liberated from plots by giving attention to her emotions. But for Lise emotion is a distraction from the dynamic of her plot, and is therefore to be avoided. She is friendly, however, to the elderly lady she meets outside her hotel: ' "It was very kind of you to come along with me" says Mrs Fiedke, "as it's so confusing in a strange place. Very kind indeed." "Why shouldn't I be kind?" Lise says, smiling at her with a sudden gentleness' (p. 81). For a moment we see warmth and softness, apparently altruistic alternatives to the hard, causal world Lise creates for herself. But immediately this kindliness is made to seem a lapse, an aberration, and is swiftly incorporated into part of a purposeful plot: ' "One should always be kind," Lise says, "in case it might be the last chance. One might be killed crossing the street, or even on the pavement, any time, you never know" ' (pp. 81–2). The plot is relentless, and Lise denies herself spontaneity or disinterested action in order to comply with it. She also denies herself grief, and this is made worse for her in that she is aware of her loss. At one point she says, 'I want to go home, I think. I want to go back home and feel all that lonely grief again. I miss it so much already' (p. 143). She does not allow herself to spend time amending this loss, since emotion is irrelevant to the outcome of the plot – indeed, it would subvert it – and it is only after Lise's death that emotion can be mentioned in all seriousness.

The last few lines of *The Driver's Seat* are very significant. The language of the novel up to this point has been spare, highly controlled, only occasionally breaking into lyricism to imply the existence of 'the possible other case'.[14] But after Lise's murder it is as if the completion of her own end-directed plot allows the narrator to assume control again, to name explicitly the feelings that have been evoked throughout the novel but ruthlessly suppressed by the protagonist herself, aided and abetted by the author. The prose becomes liberated, less distant and less hygienic; strong emotions are named and finally admitted. After he kills Lise, her murderer 'sees already the gleaming buttons of the policemen's uniforms, hears the cold and the confiding, the hot and the barking voices, sees already the holsters and epaulets and all those trappings devised to protect them from the indecent exposure of fear and pity, pity and fear' (p. 160). The Aristotelian formula reminds us, if we need reminding, that the novel is a tragedy of a woman who dies a violent death. Without parents, lovers, husband, close friends – in fact any relationship which furnishes constant drama and interest – Lise is reduced to making drama out of the most elemental plot of all, the knowledge that her life will end. Having no other purpose for her poor life, she makes her design the ending of it, and curiously, the energy and zest with which she goes about it are not completely negated by their being self-destructive. But it is only at the end of *The Driver's Seat*, when 'pity and fear' are finally stated openly, that we realise their relevance, and thus their nagging omission from the whole story. Cunningly, with bleak triumph, Mrs Spark has thoroughly implicated us in the callousness of Lise's world, a world surviving by the tacit acceptance of outward appearances as a basis of judgement. The novel says a great deal about 'trappings' of one kind or another: books are bought because their covers match a colour-scheme, people are evaluated by their clothes, and the 'trappings' of policemen, their uniforms endorsing their public image, are worn to help them to be aloof from human feelings. In the same way, the 'trappings' of the novel – the reflexiveness, the flash-forwards, the revelation of the intricate apparatus of the fictional process – all are devices which may insulate us, the readers, from emotional reaction to Lise's tragedy. But having exposed her readers to the same temptation to which she exposes Lise – that is, of accepting horror without protest for the sake of a satisfactory pattern – Mrs Spark allows us, at least, a means of salvation. And that is to realise with what painful irony she calls the expression of emotion 'indecent exposure', the words both suggesting and deploring the necessity of keeping emotions within decent and familiar bounds, and not accosting strangers with their disturbing display.

Not to Disturb continues the theme where *The Driver's Seat* ends. Lister, who is the surrogate novelist of *Not to Disturb*, takes his employers' deaths as his starting-point and prepares a fiction for use after the event. Like Lise, he takes over the organisation of the plot, and he turns messy human events into clean patterns. The novel is filled with jargon relating to the manufacture of fictions, the welding together of events; it sounds, collectively, like an extract from a thesaurus: 'coalesce', 'coincidence', 'connect', 'construe', 'co-ordinate', 'correspond'. Lister's ability to do all these things is admired by the other servants: ' "... Lister never disparates, he symmetrises", Heloise says and lights a cigarette. Pablo goes to the window and looks out at the fog. "Lister's got equibalance," he says, "and what's more, he pertains" ' (p. 95).

Lister himself is highly concerned with form: 'To put it squarely, as I say in my memoir, the eternal triangle has come full circle' (p. 39), he says in explanation of the deaths of his employers. He imposes a fictional structure on his employers' lives by assuming an end – 'The End' – and directing evidence towards it. Throughout the novel, Lister is on his guard against contingency. He says (much as E. M. Forster does in *Aspects of the Novel*), 'There is a vast difference between events that arise from and those that merely follow after each other. Those that arise are preferable' (p. 111). He copes with unforeseen events by swiftly incorporating them into his plot; 'one foresees the unforeseen' (p. 109) he says smugly. Thus when he discovers that the idiot in the attic is the Baron's heir, and not merely a distant relative of the Baroness, he has him married to a pregnant housemaid, so that the outcome of the plot remains in his control. That there is a clergyman available who has previously been summoned to the house in the middle of the night for a different reason is a deliberately 'novelistic' coincidence which Lister gleefully seizes upon: 'It's a special case Reverend. You can't refuse. In fact, you may not refuse' (p. 112). Lister's 'characters', like novelist's characters, have no choice. Anything or anyone who cannot be accommodated in his plot is eliminated from the story. When two visitors make themselves a nuisance by refusing to leave the estate (and the narrative) Lister enquires of one of the other servants who they are: ' "I didn't ask." "You did right", Lister says. "They don't come into the story" ' (p. 51). Later someone says, 'Forget them . . . they're only extras' (p. 142). And so they are. When they persist in interrupting the train of events, the narrator helps Lister by eliminating them in a subordinate clause: 'Meanwhile the lightning, which strikes the clump of elms so that the two friends huddled there are killed instantly without pain, zig-zags across the lawns, illuminating the lily pond and the sunken rose-garden . . .' (p. 143). They are allowed to die in a highly unrealistic manner – 'instantly without pain' – since they are fictional devices only. Pain would be too human; it would sully the smooth prose and delay the swift undeviating impetus of the plot. This callousness is, of course, a literary joke about the novelist's process of selection and rejection, but it is callous for all that. It reduces people to mere fictional components, tiny little constructs of words to be fitted into the text or not, as the author decides. Inevitably all authors make such a selection, but it is the gratuitous display of power, the revelling in it, which makes this incident so peculiarly disagreeable.

Artifice is the theme of this novel, and such a viewpoint has an effect on the ostensibly realistic happenings within the narrative. Although the novel follows certain Aristotelian principles laid down for drama (five 'acts', unity of time and place), Mrs Spark makes certain the action does not evoke pity and fear. In *Not to Disturb* Lister treats life as if it were a formal fictional construct, and therefore emotions can have no place in his plot. Although there are several violent deaths in the novel, the idea of tragedy is kept at arm's length by keeping the doomed employers as remote characters, whose role is merely to die in order to provide a stimulus for the fiction Lister is making. For him their deaths are central to his plot, and so, although it is known that murder and suicide will be committed, no attempt is made to prevent this, since that would spoil Lister's preconceived role as author. The servants' lack of concern at this is worrying. Restrained by the narrator from intervention, they become webbed in the indifference of the prose, and it is this indifference which becomes a matter for our attention. In *The Driver's Seat* Lise's desire for self-destruction was not sufficiently understood by the other characters for their inaction to become a moral issue. But in *Not to Disturb* the characters acquiesce in the plot. What is happening here is the overt dominance of text over agents, plot over character. If Lister and the servants tacitly allow their 'characters' to die, Mrs Spark is also involved in their quiescence, since in this novel there is very little shift in viewpoint between narrator and protagonist, and almost the only ironic distancing from the narration is the title, *Not to Disturb*. It *is* a disturbing book, and what is more disturbing about it is the change from Mrs Spark's earlier condemnation of plotters such as Patrick Seton. At this stage of her work, as I suggested in Chapter 1, her satiric stance evokes less and less the positive qualities it should conjure up. Instead, it becomes a sufficient account of the world as she sees it, a sardonic admission that for most people worldly plots do indeed take precedence over God's plot. In her early novels this was cause for regret. Here, it is stated, unembellished, merely as a matter of fact.

One of the most disquieting elements of *Not to Disturb* is Lister's impassivity, his disinterested participation in ensuring that his plot runs smoothly. In contrast, the protagonist of *Loitering with Intent* is exuberant about her powers of creativity, and through her Mrs Spark looks at the problems (and the joy) of creating plots in the capacity of a novelist. In this book she resolves her ambiguity towards the plotter as protagonist by making her heroine, Fleur Talbot, a distinguished novelist, who, as such, is granted approval for pursuing her vocation. She seems closely to resemble Mrs Spark herself, and many of her pronouncements on writing are echoes, almost word for word, of statements made by Mrs Spark in interviews. They ring true, and their validity, independent of their context within the novel, underlines the theme of *Loitering with Intent*: the peculiar truth of fiction, and its capacity to pre-empt fact.

Fleur Talbot, now a famous novelist, looks back at the time of writing her first novel in London in the late forties. Before the publication of her novel she worked for Sir Quentin Oliver, who has founded the Autobiographical Association. This consists of a group of people writing their confidential memoirs for publication after seventy years. Fleur is employed to type and, where she thinks necessary, to rewrite these memoirs. Fleur realises that Sir Quentin is behaving uncannily like Warrender Chase, the protagonist of her novel, who exercises a malign influence over a group of weak people, driving them to madness and suicide. A member of the Autobiographical Association does in fact kill herself, and Fleur discovers that Sir Quentin has been handing out drugs which are meant as appetite suppressors, but which affect the brain. He believes that in *Warrender Chase* Fleur has written about him, and he tries to destroy her typescript. He also persuades Fleur's publisher not to publish the book, on the grounds that it is libellous. In her novel, Warrender Chase is killed suddenly in a car-crash, and Quentin also suffers this fate. Fleur, having described him as 'pure evil' is thankful for his death. Her novel is accepted by a more prestigious publisher, and Fleur begins a notable career as a novelist: 'Goodbye, my poverty, goodbye, my youth' (p. 220).

Throughout *Loitering with Intent*, Fleur's novel *Warrender Chase* and the events of her daily life are interwoven. Her novel does not reflect her experiences, however; rather, it predicts them. We are told that Fleur 'rejoiced in seeing people as they were, and not only that, but more than ever as they were, and more, and more' (p. 9). In straightforward terms this means that the novelist's perception of people can, in effect, ensure a reasonably accurate prediction of their subsequent actions, so that the resulting novel becomes a prophetic rather than a retrospective account of events. Fleur realises that Sir Quentin embodies the worst qualities of her protagonist: 'In my febrile state of creativity I saw before my eyes how Sir Quentin was revealing himself chapter by chapter to be a type and consummation of Warrender Chase, my character. I could see that the members of the Autobiographical Association were about to become his victims, psychological Jack the Ripper as he was' (p. 60). In the interview with Malcolm Muggeridge Mrs Spark confirms the prophetic abilities of the novelist in real life: 'sometimes I invent a character that I meet later on after the book's written'.[15] This 'conjuring up' of characters has a Mephistophelean or blasphemous ring about it, but in *Loitering with Intent* Mrs Spark makes clear that the creative imagination of the artist (whether or not real characters or events subsequently confirm its authenticity) is in a different moral category from the deliberate meddling in people's lives practised by the 'lay' fiction-makers or manipulators, such as Sir Quentin Oliver. Fleur admits that she has invented material for the autobiographies in the course of her work for the Autobiographical Association, but she makes a distinction between her activities – on paper – and those of Sir Quentin in reality. 'It was precisely because I'd found all their biographies so very dull to start with that I'd given them so light-hearted a turn, almost as if the events they described had happened to me, not to them. . . . I was sure that nothing had happened in their lives and equally sure that Sir Quentin was pumping something artificial into their real lives instead of on paper' (pp. 116–17). This kind of exercise of power is condemned in *Loitering with Intent* as it was in Mrs Spark's early novels. While Lister and the Abbess of Crewe in later narratives were given the tacit support of the narrator, Sir Quentin is described as evil and eventually eliminated as swiftly as the innocent intruders in *Not to Disturb*. A moral emphasis re-emerges at this stage in Mrs Spark's work, almost as if a novel set in the late forties cannot be offered with the apparent neutrality characteristic of the 1970s, and typical of Mrs Spark's fiction of that period.

As in *The Comforters* Mrs Spark extends the theme of *Loitering with Intent* – the relation between fiction and reality – to the point of undermining the plot itself. While Sir Quentin's activities are presented realistically and Warrender Chase is undoubtedly a character in a novel written by Fleur, there are, nevertheless, little narratorial jokes about the relative realistic status of the two protagonists. Fleur reflects, 'It was almost as if Sir Quentin was unreal and I had merely invented him, Warrender Chase being a man, a real man on whom I had partly based Sir Quentin. It is true that I felt tight-strung, but I remember those sensations very clearly' (pp. 182–3). Mrs Spark does not let her reflexive speculation rest here, however, but extends it even to the realism of her narrator. At one point Fleur is made to doubt her own existence: 'For a moment I felt like a grey figment, the "I" of a novel whose physical description the author had decided not to set forth. I was still, of course, weak from my 'flu' (p. 95). Of course. But as it happens Mrs Spark does not give a physical description of her narrator in *Loitering with Intent*, and the carefully included realistic explanations – tiredness, 'flu – do not detract from the function of these passages as reminders that the book, on a superficial level, is fiction. Fleur deliberately contributes to these reminders when an acquaintance criticises one of her characters in *Warrender Chase*. She answers, 'How can you say that? Marjorie is fiction, she doesn't exist' (p. 73). Later, she says of Sir Quentin and his

group, 'I could have invented him, I could have invented all of them –
the lot. I said Edwina was the only real person out of the whole
collection' (p. 106). Edwina, Quentin's mother, is indeed the most
convincing and lovingly depicted character in the book, apart from
Fleur herself, and in comparison the other characters do seem
somewhat 'flat'. It is a measure of Mrs Spark's insistence on the
profound truth-telling qualities of the novel that she dares to draw
attention to its fictiveness. If the reader dismisses the surface narrative
as untrue, there remains the underlying myth, of which a particular
narrative is but one expression. In *Loitering with Intent* Mrs Spark
explains that 'Without a mythology, a novel is nothing. The true
novelist, one who understands the work as a continuous poem, is a
myth-maker, and the wonder of the art resides in the endless different
ways of telling a story, and the methods are mythological by nature'
(p. 141). The essential truth of myth is not diminished but emphasised
if its allegoric expression is shown to be unrealistic. The ostensible plot
of *Loitering with Intent* is occasionally revealed as fiction by its author
in order that its true subject may be understood – that is,
paradoxically, the possibility of truth-telling through the medium of a
novel.

Fleur's momentary doubts about her existence do not, in fact,
demolish the reader's belief in her, since she surpasses even the Abbess
of Crewe as the most joyful of all Mrs Spark's protagonists. What
comes through most forcefully is Fleur's absolute certainty of herself
as an artist. 'Such as I am, I'm an artist, not a reporter' (p. 153).
Success or failure, or being liked for her work, are by-products only:
'I wasn't writing poetry or prose so that the reader would think me a
nice person, but in order that my sets of words should convey ideas of
truth and wonder, as indeed they did to myself as I was composing
them' (p. 82). Mrs Spark's tone in this novel is so confident that such
a statement, in the context of Fleur's approach to her vocation, seems
neither high-flown nor pretentious, but simply a statement of fact.
'How wonderful it feels to be an artist and a woman in the twentieth
century' (p. 25), Fleur says. The mature novelist as narrator looks
back at her youthful artistic enthusiasm without the slightest trace of
condescension or amusement, since it is clear that her attitude towards
her vocation is still that of eagerness and wonder. In creating a first-
person narrator so closely resembling her own persona Mrs Spark has
achieved a superb portrait of an artist rejoicing in her own powers.
Indeed, 'rejoicing' is the motif of this novel. Fleur rereads Benvenuto
Cellini's *Autobiography*, and Mrs Spark includes several quotations

from it, ending with a line which recurs throughout *Loitering with Intent*: 'I am now going on my way rejoicing' (p. 127). Fleur has cause to rejoice, since, unlike Lise or Lister, she is allowed to exercise both her ability to construct a plot, and her capacity for emotion; 'to be an artist and a woman', not merely an artist. And, unlike Mrs Spark's cruder manipulators, Fleur is portrayed with a warmth of feeling and affection unprecedented in Mrs Spark's work. She has convincing friendships, and her relationship with Quentin's elderly, eccentric and incontinent mother is tender but very funny. Her deepest feelings, however, are reserved for a friend, now dead, who helped her during her early years as a novelist: 'But is is Solly Mendelsohn I mourn for. Solly, clumping and limping over Hampstead Heath with his large night-pale face. Oh Solly, my friend, my friend' (p. 221). As with Annabel Christopher, the admission of emotion gives Fleur a dignity and humanity lacking in those characters to whom it is denied. Fleur constructs plots, but she lives first. As her plots, in turn, come alive, it is an indication of the vitality with which she has bestowed them, and not, as in the case of Lise, an abnegation of life itself.

6 Structure and Style

The structure, style and content of a novel are, of course, inseparable, and this is particularly obvious in Mrs Spark's work since she uses the novel form not merely to impose coherence but to express her perception of it. As I said in Chapter 1, this is unusual for a twentieth-century writer, and it has to do with her religious beliefs. It is significant that Muriel Spark resisted writing a novel until after her conversion, which gave her a sense of unity: 'from that time I began to see life as a whole rather than as a series of disconnected happenings'.[1] This view is simultaneously that of an artist, who sees the possibility of imaginative sense from apparent randomness, and Mrs Spark seized on the connection she perceived between God's unifying purpose and that of the novelist, and put it at the centre of her work. As a Christian, she sees nothing anachronistic about this. Rather, it acts as a highly economic device, since it enables her to employ the act of writing, and the novel form, not only as potent analogues in themselves, but also to reinforce at the same time what she has to say within the novel's covers. In her view both God and the novelist create a world which they then people with characters simultaneously free and limited. Sometimes in real life characters fight back at an awareness of divine omniscience, and Mrs Spark includes in her plots a dynamic relationship between creator and characters. A further similarity between divine and novelistic structure is the perpetual relationship between the causal and the contingent. Mrs Spark has said, 'I believe events are providentially ordered'[2], and her novels reflect this belief in the way she makes the reader aware that her novels' events are similarly ordered. This is not to say that she denies the beauty and validity of contingency (particularly in her earliest and most recent work) but, while recognising and even rejoicing in the arbitrary appearance of random happenings, she continually reminds us of their potential in an ultimate design.

Cardinal Newman, writing about the argument from design in one of his letters, said, 'I believe in design because I believe in God; not in a God because I see design.'[3] For the novelist who is also a Catholic, truth is arrived at through what is originally an act of faith: that, because God's order is immanent, there is the artistic possibility of turning contingency into pattern.

This viewpoint appeals to Mrs Spark's sense of economy, since it means that nothing is wasted, either in real life or in the novel; what appears accidental is, in fact, purposeful. The awareness dictates the form of her novels, and it came as a relief to her because she was initially reluctant to commit herself to a genre so apparently formless in comparison with her earlier discipline as a poet: 'before I could face this question of writing a novel I had to think, "Well, what form is it? Has it got a form? What is the form for me?" '[4] The form for her is usually succinct and tightly structured, being a simultaneous demonstration of God's undeviating purpose, and the unremitting nature of the novelist's plot, but veering in emphasis from the former to the latter during the course of her work. Nevertheless, her longer, looser novels echo and endorse their themes with equal appropriateness: 'the theme that one is writing about dictates its own form . . . if there's a kind of complex — form/theme complex — then that's the most successful type of novel, if one could achieve that'.[5] *The Comforters, The Bachelors, The Mandelbaum Gate, The Takeover* and *Territorial Rights* are Mrs Spark's longest novels, and this is because they contain characters who resist the inevitability of plot and explore the contingent world, taking longer than most of Mrs Spark's characters to succumb to the ultimate causality of God and the novelist. These novels contain more descriptive passages, more dwelling on the outward scene. There is a greater narratorial generosity, but there is never a sense of total largesse; rather it is hinted that the wider the range, the wider is God's net. Even trivia, the narrator implies, will be relevant by the end of the novel.

In her shorter novels, Mrs Spark usually details the mores of a small community which acts as a microcosm of the larger world. Geriatrics, bachelors, factory workers and unmarried girls form groups, not from choice, but because of the unsought similarity of their conditions. Mrs Spark has a literary predilection for their hermetic quality, and in an interview with Frank Kermode she describes the way in which her chosen angle subsequently dictates her vision of reality:

When I become interested in a subject, say old age, then the world is peopled for me – just peopled with them. And it is a narrow little small world, but it's full of old people, full of whatever I'm studying. They're the centre of the world, and everyone else is on the periphery. It is an obsession until I've finished writing about them. And that's how I see things. I wrote a book about bachelors and it seemed to me that everyone was a bachelor.[6]

Having decided on her subject, Mrs Spark then explores it on a minute, detailed scale. This is not just a useful technique, imposing as it does confines within which to work, but a particular way of arriving at the truth. Groups themselves form patterns and fictions, as Mrs Spark interestingly observes in her book on John Masefield:

It seems to be true of any unmixed or specialist community whose members are forced to live together at close quarters, that by acknowledged, instinctive and common consent, certain events – events which may seem quite trivial – take on the features of myth, the dimensions of which increase with time and frequent communication. . . . this type of mythology is akin to tradition, but tradition is more conscious, more organized, than is this elementary and primitive instinct to 'legendarize' isolated events, and so bind together imaginatively a community already closely bound by material necessity.[7]

Mrs Spark seizes on the potentially legendary in her communities, such as the personality of Miss Brodie, or the fire at the May of Teck hostel, and encloses it in a plot of her own. We are thus given an event in three ways: first, realistically; secondly, through the eyes of the participants; and only finally endowed with the symbolism bestowed on the event by the narrator's attitude. From the meticulous chronicling of a small section of society larger truths about the virtues and frailties of human nature emerge, still sticky with realism, and not as a clean, omniscient generalisation applied from outside the events described. This is in contrast to Mrs Spark's novellas, where realism is often subordinated to a formula about the nature of the novel, making these works ultimately less satisfying than the narrow, but dense and closely observed worlds of the earlier novels.

In *Loitering with Intent* the narrator, a novelist, says, 'I conceive everything poetically' (p. 28). Muriel Spark evolved from a poet to a novelist through the practice of short-story writing, and her novels still bear this stamp. They give the impression of the novelist – God-like – seeing the end of the novel at the beginning, and Mrs Spark sometimes fuses the teleological interests of the novelist with these of eschatology by having a death at the end of the narrative. The unity of *The Driver's Seat* comes from that particular fusion, but all Mrs Spark's work suggests that she invariably has an overall view of her plot which acts as a method of control throughout the construction of the novel. This, for her, is not a slick process, but the culmination of a long period of mental gestation:

> I walk round the subject. I think of it and then I don't think of it
> . . . this goes on for a few months and I might write a few lines or I
> might not and it teases me and worries me and then by the time I
> come to write it I have a something, a sense of almost as if I'd
> finished the book so acutely that I finish it in a few weeks' time.[8]

What emerges is 'crystalline'[9] in its lack of deep characterisation and its allegoric quality. Mrs Spark eschews a broad, realistic canvas, concentrating instead on revealing the significance latent in everyday reality. She points out that 'fiction to me is a kind of parable',[10] and, although allegory is intrinsic to her work, it is scarcely a structural device – more nearly an appropriate way of denoting the sacramental nature of the world as it appears to her. So in reading her novels it is necessary to direct our attention to what the surface narratives represent. I have already mentioned the allegory immanent in her work relating to human and divine authorship, the orderly worlds of the novelist and God; sometimes this is extended. *Robinson* and *The Mandelbaum Gate* are Freudian allegories about an individual's search for unity; *The Public Image* symbolises the wider implications of self-deception, and *Not to Disturb* continues this theme by acting as an allegory of the distorting power of the media. *The Hothouse by the East River* and *The Abbess of Crewe* represent other places (purgatory and the White House) which are themselves symbolic, but in these novels the allegory is not sustained, since Mrs Spark withholds precise parallels so that it is impossible to interpret the internal symbolism. What can be found in all Mrs Spark's work is a stratum of meanings, of which the surface is emblematic only, and which invites exploration. Unless this economic structure is understood, the reader is likely to share the disappointment of the reviewer of *The Driver's Seat* in the *Times Literary Supplement*, who, having worked out that the novel 'will take you 60 minutes to read and cost you sixpence a minute',[11] gives the impression that more was expected for the money. But Mrs Spark, in effect, gives the reader two novels for the price of one. The comment Luigi makes about Annabel in *The Public Image* can also be applied to her author: 'Her talent, he thought, is a rich one. As in life, he thought, it is the very rich who understand thrift while the poor spend quickly on trifles' (p. 144).

The structure of Mrs Spark's novels is affected by her attitude to the concept of time, and her consequent handling of tenses and time-span within her narratives. In *Myths, Dreams and Mysteries* Mircea Eliade examines the relationship between primitive beliefs and contemporary faiths, and he points out that 'Christianity . . . has had to preserve at least one mythic attitude – the attitude towards liturgical time; that is, the rejection of profane time'.[12] Mrs Spark, too, rejects profane or chronological time as an adequate metaphor for conveying her awareness of the world *sub specie aeternitatis*, and the more perceptive of her characters realise the everlasting status of momentary actions. Caroline, in *The Comforters*, says, 'the next few eternal minutes are important' (p. 31), accepting the eschatological implications in time present. Thus tenses can be used unconventionally in Mrs Spark's novels to convey more than past, present and future. In her early novels she uses the conventional past tense (although she makes it quite clear that she knows it is a convention), but even in her first novel she displays an impatient briskness when dealing with time, compressing a century or so of history in a sentence. She describes Louisa Jepp's ancestry, her descent for a successful gypsy corn-dealer:

> The success was owing to good fortune in the first place, his having broken jail while waiting to come before the Bench, never afterwards returning to his gypsy tribe. It was a hundred and thirty years after this event that Louisa was sitting down to breakfast with Laurence. (p. 7)

In *The Driver's Seat* Mrs Spark begins her use of the present tense, with flash-forwards in the determined future tense to emphasise that Lise's future is already determined. The present tense gives immediacy and tension to the plot, and an illusion of spontaneous action. In this novel it is also used as an economic method of demonstrating Lise's rootlessness, her lack of a significant past, her ahistorical function as a component in a novel. In *Not to Disturb* the perception of time is made the subject of jokes by the God-like butler

Lister. When someone mentions that he will see the Baron in the morning, Lister says, ' "Too late ... the Baron is no more." "I can hear his voice. What d'you mean?" "Let us not strain after vulgar chronology", says Lister' (p. 66).

'Vulgar chronology' is Mrs Spark's view of chronological time, and for her the act of writing is in itself what she has called 'an attempt to redeem the time'.[13] Through her writing the experience of everyday happenings is captured, refined and rendered into a statement of moral sense. In an article on Proust she quotes his agnostic opinion that only art gives point and permanence to the ephemeral: ' "Time as it flows", he wrote "is so much time wasted and nothing can ever be truly possessed save under that aspect of eternity which is also the aspect of art." Lacking a redemptive faith, Proust's attempt was to save himself through art.'[14] This somewhat pessimistic view of what is, after all, life-time and not simply abstract time, is shared by Mrs Spark, although for her art is not seen as redemptive in itself, functioning rather as a perpetual allegory of divine redemption. Her conception of time is close to Proust's however, in that neither accepts a chronological view of time as appropriate to describe the continuum of their own and other people's lives. In her novels Mrs Spark frequently gives away the ending early on, so that the reader's interest is redirected from the simple linear suspense to the more interesting speculations of 'how?' and 'why?' There is more in heaven and earth, she implies, than simple chronology, and what emerges from the text is not a chronological but a moral order. This is particularly true of *The Prime of Miss Jean Brodie*, the sequence of which is worth examining in some detail, since it is the first and most elaborate use by Mrs Spark of flash-backs and flash-forwards. Actions, apparently trivial in themselves, are juxtaposed with their consequences or their motivation, and, thus compressed, reveal moral connections which would be unapparent in a purely sequential narrative until the end of the book. We begin to understand the connective influences of past, present and future, and the ways in which childhood and maturity predict and reflect each other.

In *The Prime of Miss Jean Brodie* there are fourteen flash-backs and fourteen flash-forwards, and gradually we build up a composite picture of the girls in their childhood, adolescence and as adults. Childish characteristics emerge in adulthood: Sandy's shrewd, youthful observation of people's behaviour, particularly Miss Brodie's, is formalised as she becomes a psychologist. Rose, fulfilling her sexual potential, but not according to Miss Brodie's plans, 'made a good marriage soon after she left school' (p. 159). Mary Macgregor, the butt of the group, dies aged twenty-three, in a blazing building. We are told this in Chapter 2 of the novel, and later, in Chapter 4, we learn that Mary panics during a science experiment at school involving spectacular flames. The science-lesson fire is in some way a prophecy of Mary's death, yet the reader learns of it after learning that her death has occurred. Our knowledge of the way Mary dies lends significance to the earlier incident; instead of a silly reaction in a science lesson it becomes a portent of Mary's fate. Her role at school is that of the 'Brodie set' scapegoat. She is 'officially the faulty one' (p. 36), and throughout the novel is depicted as clumsy, stupid and ritually blamed. As early as Chapter 2, however, we learn that for Mary her first years with Miss Brodie 'had been the happiest time of her life' (p. 15), and that after she left school she was as miserable as she should logically have been while at school. This information is disconcerting, since it weakens our sympathetic response to Mary's trials as a schoolgirl, because we know in advance that she has been less upset by them than we imagine. So strangely, the technique of the flash-forward does not necessarily render the narrative more predictable; the surprises are there, but of a different order.

We learn in Chapter 2 that there is some kind of tragedy attached to Miss Brodie's retirement, and that she has been betrayed, for some reason, by one of 'her' girls. About halfway through the novel we are told casually that it is Sandy who has betrayed Miss Brodie, and thereafter we pay greater attention to Sandy's perception of her teacher than to that of the other girls, since the action, we now realise, revolves on this. The flash-forwards often render the text ironic. For example, the first time Miss Brodie tells Sandy that she will 'go too far' (p. 27) we have no knowledge of her betrayal, and the words have little significance. The next time, however, when we learn that 'Miss Brodie looked at her as if to say . . . " One day Sandy, you will go too far for my liking" ' (p. 86), the words take on import and irony, because we now know not only of Miss Brodie's downfall, but also of Sandy's part in it. As the flash-forwards accumulate, they contribute to our knowledge of future events, and we realise that Miss Brodie's plans for the girls' destinies are not going to be fulfilled. This realisation gives us a perspective on the intensity of her activities. The reader, unlike Miss Brodie, really does see 'the beginning and the end' (p. 161). Her fantasies in the light of their subsequent failure seem megalomanic and far-fetched, although Miss Brodie's own conviction in their fruition is always convincing. This technique of flash-forwards and flash-backs reveals an order which has a formal as well as a moral transcendence; by turning contingency into necessity Mrs Spark sustains not only the purposefulness of God's world but also the coherence of the novelist's. We see clearly the aesthetic patterning involved in writing a novel, a process which in itself has always interested Mrs Spark and which, in *The Driver's Seat* and *Not to Disturb* becomes virtually the subject of the novel. In *The Prime of Miss Jean Brodie*, however, contingency and necessity have both religious and structural implications, and when Mrs Spark achieves this balance she produces her best work.

Muriel Spark's style is distinctive. Its most striking characteristic is its tone of confidence and authority, and because it radiates certainty it is highly persuasive. Yet again, it is to her religious faith that we must look for an explanation of this aspect of Mrs Spark's work. Commenting on the connection she says, 'I didn't get my style until I became a Catholic because you just haven't got to care, and you need security for that. That's the whole secret of style in a way. It's simply not caring too much, it's caring only a little.'[15] In her later novels the word 'style' is used by characters in a way which increasingly goes beyond the meaning of mere 'stylishness'. In *The Hothouse by the East River* Princess Xavier, the most sensible person in the novel, says 'I believe in style' (p. 104), and in *The Abbess of Crewe* Alexandra uses 'style' as an indication of what she considers to be good breeding: 'A Lady has style; but a Bourgeoise does things under the poplars and in the orchard' (p. 89). By the time the word is used in *The Takeover* it has a moral connotation:

'You must understand that with a woman like the Marchesa everything must be done in style. If your style wavers she takes immediate advantage of it and walks all over you.' . . .

'Style, style', said Massimo de Vita grasping at the idea as if it were a crust, and he starving for it, as indeed he was. . . . He thought, in fact, that he exercised a quality which he called style, but was in reality an aggressive cynicism. Style, in the sense that he believed himself to possess it, needs a certain basic humility; and without it there can never be any distinction of manner or of anything whatsoever. (p. 177)

The somewhat paradoxical idea of style needing humility links with Mrs Spark's account of her own style quoted above, and with her declared intention of 'writing minor novels deliberately, and not major novels'.[16] And, indeed, there is a lightness of tone, a lack of hectoring, in Muriel Spark's work which makes her all the more convincing, since the reader is scarcely aware of the process of persuasion.

The word 'economy' runs through Mrs Spark's novels. Sandy Stranger admires the economical methods of both Miss Brodie and Teddy Lloyd, and 'it always seemed afterwards to Sandy that where there was a choice of various courses, the most economical was the best' (p. 135). In *The Takeover* we are told that a character has 'an intuitive artistic sense of economy' (p. 33), and this applies also to Mrs Spark. It derives partly from her earlier discipline as a poet, where every word had to earn its keep or be eliminated. Not surprisingly, she admires the laconic style of the Scottish Border ballads, and something of their resonant understatement characterises her novels. She talks about this reticence in an interview:

> I do think that if I manage to convey another dimension in my books it is between the lines. I don't ever say that there is something mysterious going on here. I try not to hope that all this other dimension is sort of read between the lines, and I think that effect can be achieved in a purely methodical and technical way by keeping out as much comment as possible.[17]

Muriel Spark's story 'The Go-Away Bird' is a useful illustration of her economical method of conveying meaning 'between the lines'. Her heroine, Daphne du Toit, grows up in Africa just before the Second World War. She lives with her guardian, who is English but is known by his African name, Chakata. As the result of an ancient feud between Chakata and his Dutch tobacco-manager, Old Tuys, Daphne's life is constantly threatened, and she survives two attempts at her murder. Daphne longs to go to England, but her departure is prevented by the war. She eventually sails in 1946, and learns that England contains people quite as dangerous as Old Tuys, however well their savagery is disguised. She is exploited by a rapacious society woman, and by a novelist called Ralph Mercer with whom she has an affair. After two years with Ralph he tells her to leave and she returns to Africa. Chakata is now almost bedridden with rheumatism, and Old Tuys, his mind wandering, is now considered harmless. But he shoots Daphne, mistaking her for a buck, and ironically he achieves his revenge on Chakata without realising it.

A year after Daphne's death Ralph feels that his books are not being taken seriously enough, and decides to write a tragedy using her short life and sudden death as material. He visits Africa to seek out her background, and is fêted by the Europeans there. So much so that he decides to buy a farm in the colony to use for part of the year. He goes to Daphne's grave, where he hears for the first time the bird she had often told him about: ' "Go 'way, go 'way", said the bird behind Daphne's grave' (p. 358). After this he too is able to distinguish the bird-cry from the general noise of the bush, and it haunts him. He decides not to buy the farm after all, and returns to England, unable to exploit Daphne's death as he exploited her during her lifetime.

Although 'The Go-Away Bird' is a dramatic story its tone is dispassionate, its diction precise, and its effects are achieved with the utmost economy. The opening paragraph introduces the 'go-away' bird, whose call encapsulates the theme of rejection which, although unstated, runs through the narrative:

> All over the Colony it was possible to hear the subtle voice of the grey-crested lourie, commonly known as the go-away bird by its call, 'go 'way, go 'way'. It was possible to hear the bird, but very few did, for it was part of the background to everything, a choir of birds and beasts, the crackle of vegetation in the great prevalent sunlight, and the soft rhythmic pad of natives, as they went barefoot and in single-file, from kraal to kraal.
>
> (*Collected Stories I*, p. 302)

Daphne's romantic longing for all things English turns the bird-cry into a message for her. But, ironically, she hears the same words from a bird in England, when a talking budgerigar tells her to 'Go 'way, go to hell' (p. 342). Mrs Spark never uses the word 'hell' as a mere colloquialism, and it is a hint that Daphne's life does indeed resemble it. When Ralph in turn tells her to 'go away' we are given a direct indication of her feelings for the first time: 'Now, after two years her passion for him was not diminished, neither were her misery and dread' (p. 351). In this way, Daphne's unhappiness is not dramatised, but stated flatly and in negative terms. There is no further elaboration of her feelings. We learn that on returning to Africa she finds Chakata and Old Tuys tacitly reconciled through infirmity and old age. Then, with apparent casualness, and without the narrator heralding it as a revelation, an appalling sentence is inserted between a description of Tuys's eating habits and Daphne's desire for a job: 'It struck Daphne that she was useless to Chakata now that she was no longer a goad for Old Tuys' (p. 353). In other words, her guardian valued her not for herself, but only as long as her existence was an irritant to his enemy. Looking back through the text, this is confirmed by Chakata's letters to Daphne in England, which neither she, nor the reader, can understand at the time:

> Earlier Chakata had written, 'Old Tuys has had a stroke. He is up now, but very feeble in his mind.' Since then, he had seemed less keen on Daphne's return. Daphne thought this odd, for previously he had been wont to write when sending her news of the farm, 'You will see many changes when you return', or, when mentioning affairs at the dorp, 'There's a new doctor. You'll like him.' But in his last letter he had said, 'There have been changes in the educational system. You will find many changes if you return.' (p. 345)

Daphne's realisation of Chakata's lack of feeling for her confirms her worthlessness in the eyes of other people, even those whom she loves. The climax of her misery, and of the story, comes when she goes for a walk in the bush and sits down to rest. ' "Go 'way. Go 'way", she heard. Daphne called aloud, "God help me. Life is unbearable" ' (p. 353). Her sudden utterance of despair sums up the rootless and loveless quality of her entire life. It is the only time in the narrative that she prays for help, and help of a kind is immediately at hand. Her prayer is answered, very literally. She is shot by Old Tuys, and relieved of her suffering. This very Catholic logic is perhaps disconcerting, but there is no doubt that, in view of what has gone before, the reader is meant to see Daphne's death as a good answer to her prayer.

Because 'The Go-Away Bird' is written in a matter-of-fact tone, Daphne's cry of total desolation is at first surprising. In the preceding narrative she has been portrayed as a somewhat passive figure, greatly exploited, frequently using the phrase 'Oh I see' to cover her embarrassment, shock or misery. The level tone reflects Daphne's quiescent acceptance of other people's cruelty to her, and in this way (as she does later in *The Driver's Seat*) Mrs Spark lures the reader into accepting the outrageous treatment of the heroine as a matter of course. There is virtually no narratorial comment to help the reader

take sides. Only three times in this long short story does the narrator
hint very briefly that there is an alternative world, acknowledgement
of which might force us to refocus our viewpoint of the realistic
events described. First, the mention of hell, ostensibly as a stock
phrase. Secondly, the quotation from a popular song, which Daphne
happily dances to in the arms of a man who is deceiving her: 'The
fundamental things apply/As time goes by' (p. 325). Here, as in *The
Girls of Slender Means*, the lyric of a fashionable tune is taken out of
context, and revitalised by being used as an oblique reminder that
eternal values persist. The final hint we are given that the material
world is not all-important is the reaction of Ralph and his mother to
the news of Daphne's death. Ralph considers that Daphne only really
began to live under his influence, and therefore was in a sense already
dead after she had gone back to Africa. He tries to explain this
appallingly arrogant view to his mother, using a Berkeleian analogy:
' "Like flowers, you know, in a garden. One can't say they really
exist unless one's looking at them. Or take –" "Flowers, garden …
You are talking of a human soul" ' (p. 355). Ralph's mother sums up
the import of this story. Mrs Spark in portraying Daphne's short, sad
life is not merely giving us a study of deception and disillusion, but
'talking of a human soul'. Daphne is materially well provided for, but
emotionally and spiritually she is desolate, and her death is, quite
literally, her salvation.

Most of Mrs Spark's work successfully conveys 'another
dimension' through techniques of precision and economy, but in each
of her novels she occasionally employs an alternative style which, in
comparison, is lyrical and extravagant. Jonathan Raban, in an article
on Evelyn Waugh, makes the point that his work shows two distinct
styles: the flat, child-like observations characteristic of *Decline and
Fall* and *Vile Bodies*, and 'another style…. Self-consciously "grown-
up", with its magisterial periods and elaborate parallelisms, . . . a style
which Waugh reserved (in his fiction) for speaking about country
houses, history and the Church.'[18] Mrs Spark does something similiar.
The predominant tone of her novels, although not 'child-like', is
apparently simple, with short words and concise sentences. But she is
capable of a kind of passionate lyricism, using longer and more
complicated sentences, to convey her affirmation of what is being
stated. This in her earlier novels is usually to do with religion,
although in her later work she tranfers this style to secular subjects,
such as the description of money in *The Takeover* quoted in Chapter 4.
In *Memento Mori* the Last Rites are described, and the prose becomes

slower in pace, and reiterative, the process of thought expressed
becoming almost a meditation in itself:

> Miss Valvona's tears dropped into her supper. She was thinking
> of her father's Last Sacrament, after which he had recovered to live
> a further six months. The priest behind the screen would be
> committing Granny Barnacle to the sweet Lord, he would be
> anointing Granny Barnacle's eyes, ears, nose, mouth, hands and
> feet, asking pardon for the sins she had committed by sight, by
> hearing, smell, taste and speech, by the touch of her hands, and by
> her very footsteps.
> The priest left. A few of the patients finished their supper. Those
> who did not were coaxed with Ovaltine. At seven the sister took a
> last look behind the screen before going off to the dining room.
> 'How is she now?' said a granny.
> 'Sleeping nicely.'   (p. 125)

The contrast is self-evident. The affirmative prose leaves with the
priest, as it were, and the ordinary world reasserts itself. The
heightened language is Mrs Spark's sudden, open expression of
'another dimension' previously conveyed between the lines.
Significantly, her novels invariably end with such a passage. This is
partly to confirm the values implied but left unsaid within the novel,
as in *The Driver's Seat* and *The Public Image*, but also because the
ending of the novel somehow makes it safe for Mrs Spark to be
extravagant, since there will be no further demands on her high and
lavish style.

Calling upon these two styles Mrs Spark is capable of achieving a
wide range of effects, but they are united by a remarkable consistency
of tone in each novel. She says of this, 'I am intent on getting a tone
of writing suitable for a theme – this means that I (very personally)
have to get into an actual frame of mind which corresponds to the
theme.'[19] Of all Mrs Spark's novels, perhaps the one which is most
consistent is *The Prime of Miss Jean Brodie*. The narrative voice is
precise and authoritative and faintly pedantic, exactly right for a story
about an Edinburgh schoolmistress in the 'thirties. In addition, the
narrator is given other registers where appropriate: biblical language
is used to imply and alert us to religious parallels; schoolgirl jargon
abounds, not simply in the mouths of the girls themselves, but as part
of the narration. For example, we are told at the beginning of the

novel that the girls in Miss Brodie's set are each 'famous' for something – sex-appeal, mathematics, gymnastics – the tone being one of breathless, schoolgirlish enthusiasm slightly reminiscent of Angela Brazil. When Sandy has tea with the Lloyds the narrator says factually, 'The Lloyds were Catholics and so were made to have a lot of children by force' (p. 135). This is obviously Sandy's viewpoint, but the statement is made without mitigating quotation marks or attribution. A similar technique is used to convey the puritan attitudes of Edinburgh. Miss Brodie teaches her girls 'the advantages to the skin of cleansing cream and witch hazel over honest soap and water' – the adjective 'honest' conveying Edinburgh's approbation of plain soap and water and disapproval of Miss Brodie's alternatives. We are also told that 'Sandy's mother had a flashy winter coat trimmed with fluffy fox fur like the Duchess of York's, while the other mothers wore tweed or, at the most, musquash that would do them all their days' (p. 19). 'Flashy' and 'fluffy' are, in this context, clearly condemnatory, representing the Edinburgh view of such fashions, while the monosyllabic, functional description of musquash echoes precisely the puritanism it describes. Such details, unobtrusive and often unremarked, recur in Mrs Spark's fiction, and illustrate her unerring skill in fitting form to theme.

The Ballad of Peckham Rye also reflects its theme, stylistically, its bald narration stating the flat, dull quality of Peckham life. One of the funniest – and saddest – scenes in the novel is an account of two lovers spending Midsummer's evening together. Instead of the romantic idyll this suggests, the affair is dull in the extreme, a frightening wasteland of stale and unloving habit. Here is Mrs Spark's description of Merle and Mr Druce waiting for their meal to finish cooking:

> 'The Brussels are not quite ready', she said, and she sat in her chair and took up her knitting. He perched on the arm. She pushed him with her elbow in the same movement as she was using for her knitting. He tickled the back of her neck, which she put up with for a while. (p. 69)

The grim hilarity this scene evokes is due to the equal emphasis on each detail. We realise, without being told, that Mr Druce's passion is on a par with partly cooked Brussels sprouts, and later, after the couple have made love, the scene ends unromantically and with typical Sparkian bathos: 'She went into the scullery and put on the kettle while he put on his trousers and went home to his wife' (p. 71).

This ability to make prose enact what it is describing is honed in the course of Mrs Spark's work. In *The Girls of Slender Means* Mrs Spark describes Jane Wright's misery: she is overweight and underpaid, and, in addition, she knows only too well that Nicholas's attentions to her are primarily to ensure his acquaintance with Selina, who is slim and beautiful:

> He said, 'Tell me again that delightful thing Selina repeats about poise.'
> 'Poise is perfect balance, an equanimity of body and mind, complete composure whatever the social scene. Elegant dress, immaculate ... Oh, Christ,' she said, 'I'm so tired of picking crumbs of meat out of the shepherd's pie, picking with a fork to get the little bits of meat separated from the little bits of potato. You don't know what it's like trying to eat enough to live on and at the same time avoid fats and carbohydrates.'   (p. 82)

The contrast between Selina's elegant life and Jane's dreary existence needs no further comment from the narrator. The language of Jane's description reflects the fiddly, complex process she is describing. Later in the same novel Mrs Spark dwells on the irritating mannerisms of Jarvie, one of the club's older spinsters, and allows us to see how they affect Jane:

> Jarvie smoothed them [her gloves] out on her lap, then fluttered her fingers over the cuffs, turning them back. . . . Jarvie surveyed her gloves' irremovable utility mark with her head at a slight angle, as if considering some question connected with it. She then smoothed out the gloves again and jerkily adjusted her spectacles. Jane felt in a great panic to get married.   (p. 96)

Again, the reader is expected to make the connection between Jarvie's fidgeting and Jane's panic, without being given the linking thought-processes. Clearly Jane is terrified by the thought of becoming like Jarvie if she does not marry. A later spinster in Mrs Spark's canon is much more frightening, and her description of Lise in *The Driver's Seat* illustrates the way her prose can conjure up a mood or atmosphere through diction and syntax that seemingly bears only on the explicit subject.

Her lips are slightly parted; she, whose lips are usually pressed together with the daily disapprovals of the accountants' office where she has worked continually, except for the months of illness, since she was eighteen, that is to say, for sixteen years and some months. Her lips, when she does not speak or eat, are normally pressed together like the ruled line of a balance sheet, marked straight with her old-fashioned lipstick, a final and a judging mouth, a precision instrument, a detail-warden of a mouth; she has five girls under her and two men. Over her are two women and five men. (p. 12)

On first reading, there is a clear, paraphrasable content. Lise is thirty-four years old, although the information is given indirectly by the narrator as if parodying yet submitting to the convention of evasiveness some women practise on this subject. She has worked in the same accountants' office for sixteen years, since she was eighteen, although she does not find it particularly congenial. At one point in her career she has had an illness requiring some months off work. She is midway in the office hierarchy, where there are more senior men than women, and more junior girls than men. But we also learn, indirectly, about Lise's character through the almost obsessive emphasis (seven references in three sentences) on her lips and mouth. They are described with a relentless repetition of simile and metaphor, so that the picture that comes over of Lise's personality is far more detailed than at first perceived. She is normally highly controlled, since even to part her lips slightly is a sign of unusual animation. There is also the connotation of frigidity here. The colour of her lipstick indicates that she is indifferent to current fashions, and suggests that she does not bother to make herself look attractive. Her mouth habitually expresses disapproval, and one imagines that her judgements will be final and inflexible. It is implied that no mistake gets by without comment: 'a detail-warden of a mouth; she has five girls under her and two men'. The semi-colon linking two apparently disparate sentences emphasises syntactically the dominance Lise exercises over her subordinates. Although this is the narrator's description of Lise, the controlled, compressed, rather jerky prose is almost how one imagines Lise herself would write, and some of her neurotic quality seems to have infected her description. As far as the plot is concerned, the most important fact that the reader needs to know is that Lise has had a mysterious illness requiring a long absence from work, but this vital clue is almost hidden and the overwhelming impression conveyed by that passage is of a cold, inflexible, faintly sinister woman. She is in a situation deserving our sympathy, but her personality is such that makes it difficult to feel for her. The reader is unable to get close to Lise, and this feeling of distance reinforces our awareness of her isolation within the novel.

Moral implications lurk in Mrs Spark's prose, and a method she uses to convey them is the deliberate and often incongruous combination of her two styles, setting up situations and characters with grandeur and then deflating or deflecting the expectations aroused in the reader by her grandiloquence. In this way she reflects Max Beerbohm, an influence she acknowledges. In an article on Beerbohm's work Edmund Wilson comments on the contrast between the 'Byzantine' and the 'common-sense' nature of his style:

> In its gemminess, its artificiality, its excrescences of grotesque fancy, it sometimes becomes positively Byzantine. The Englishman in Max, on the other hand, is moderate and unassertive, dominated by common sense – and not merely correct and prosaic, but even occasionally a bit of a Philistine. . . . It was the Byzantine that pricked him to cultivate his early preciosity of style; the Englishman that taught him the trick, exploited through his whole career, of letting this preciosity down, with deprecating and comic effect, by a descent into the flatly colloquial.[20]

In Mrs Spark's work this technique conveys the gap between aspiration and achievement, between ideas of heaven and the reality of the world, and is the source of much of her comedy. For example, in *The Comforters* she describes Sir Edwin Manders thus:

> It is possible for a man matured in religion by half a century of punctilious observance, having advanced himself in devotion the slow and exquisite way, trustfully ascending his winding stair, and, to make assurance doubly sure, supplementing his meditations by deep-breathing exercises twice daily, to go into a flat spin when faced with some trouble which does not come within a familiar category. (p. 126)

She uses the deceptive, poetic power of language to reveal (showing an ironic awareness of her own ability) the fact of its deception. The slow, stately prose, its lofty metaphor and literary allusion, crashes deliberately into the colloquialism of a 'flat spin', reflecting its subject's banality and inadequacy in a sudden crisis. This stylistic precision is motivated by her acute sense always of the difference between facade and reality – Edwin's view of Edwin and God's view of Edwin – and also by the way in which language, skilfully used, can either erect facades or tear them down. Using the same method, Mrs Spark conveys the essential vulgarity of a character called Daisy Overend, in a short story of the same name:

> I am seldom in the West End of London. But sometimes I have to hurry across the Piccadilly end of Albemarle Street where the buses crash past like giant orgulous parakeets, more thunderous and more hectic than the Household Cavalry. The shops are on my left and the Green Park lies on my right under the broad countenance of drowsy summer. It is then that, in my mind's eye, Daisy Overend gads again, diminutive, charming, vicious, and tarted up to the nines. (*Collected Stories I*, p. 195)

In *The Public Image* she lends this style to the account of the image-making process surrounding Annabel Christopher:

> Within a few weeks, throughout Italy and beyond, it was decidedly understood, thoroughly suggested, hinted and memorized, that in private, inaccessible to all possible survey, and particularly in bed, Annabel Christopher, the new star who played the passionate English governess, let rip. (p. 42)

The tantalising nature of the long, involved sentence bursts out in the energetic frankness of the last two words. These colloquialisms – 'flat spin', 'tarted up to the nines', 'let rip' – explode the dignity of what has gone before. This kind of writing is based on what Mrs Spark has called the 'nevertheless idea', which permeates her work far beyond the confines of individual paragraphs:

> I believe myself to be fairly indoctrinated by the habit of thought which calls for this word. In fact I approve of the ceremonious accumulation of weather forecasts and barometer-readings that pronounce for a fine day, before letting rip on the statement: 'Nevertheless, it's raining.' I find that much of my literary composition is based on the nevertheless idea. I act upon it. It was on the nevertheless principle that I turned Catholic.[21]

She is capable of applying this principle very succinctly, using her economical style on its own, but compressing her meaning through the use of irony or *double-entendre*. The titles of her novels are often ironic, *Not to Disturb*, for instance, acting as an important directive to the reader. Her compression, like her Catholicism, takes some getting used to. In *The Bachelors* we learn about Isobel Billows: 'Isobel had been three years divorced from her husband and always said to her new friends "I was the innocent party", which they did not doubt, and the very statement of which proved, to some of her friends, that she was so in a sense' (p. 107). The economy of this description makes it resonate with implications, wittier and more pointed than if they were spelt out. Similarly, we are told in *The Prime of Miss Jean Brodie*, a girl gets killed on her way to fight in Spain, having run away from school. The narrator says that 'the school held an abbreviated form of remembrance service for her' (p. 158). By shortening her remembrance service the school is shown to question the value of the girl's impetuosity. But the reader, in turn, is led to question the implicitly censorious attitude of the school when, however muddled her motives, a child has been killed. This invitation to moral evaluation arises not from any detailed account of the rights and wrongs of the situation, but very economically from the one word 'abbreviated'. Such sharpness seems clear-sighted and laudable when directed against institutions or characters in her novels, but when our subsequent self-righteousness, as readers, is mocked in its turn, it is not so comfortable. In a reference made to Miss Brodie and the girls' romantic view of her affair with Mr Lowther, we are told, 'it was only in retrospect that they could see Miss Brodie's affair for what it was'. Here we expect the narrator to continue 'a minor affair of convenience' or 'merely a physical passion', but Mrs Spark suspends judgement, and the sentence ends 'that is to say, in a factual light' (p. 113). The reader is similarly led on in *Memento Mori*, where Mrs Spark writes,

> Lisa Brooke died in her seventy-third year after her second stroke. She had taken nine months to die, and in fact it was only a year before her death that, feeling rather ill, she had decided to reform her life, and reminding herself how attractive she still was, offered up the new idea, her celibacy to the Lord to whom no gift whatsoever is unacceptable.   (p. 15)

The idea of an old, ill woman of seventy-two offering up her celibacy to God as if it were a strenuous act of self-denial is comic, but our amusement at her vanity is thoroughly chastened by the last seven words of the paragraph, which are utterly serious. The reader seldom finishes a novel by Muriel Spark without coming under attack. In *Memento Mori*, also, we are told that 'Mrs Anthony knew instinctively that Mrs Pettigrew was a kindly woman. Her instinct was wrong' (p. 53). Even as we linger trustingly on the reliable word 'instinctively' the next sentence shatters that trust. Mrs Pettigrew's behaviour subsequently confirms the narrator's superior knowledge, and the incident seems an accurate reflection of Mrs Spark's opinion about the fallibility of human instinct.

Mrs Spark's comedy is closely related to her style. 'I have inside me a laughter demon without which I would die' (p. 19), says Hubert Mallindaine in *The Takeover*, and it would seem that this is her view also. Making people laugh, as many a comedian will confirm, is initially a defensive measure. In Mrs Spark's case, the jokes, like the smooth, invigilated prose, guard against an invasion of privacy or emotional exposure. As one critic has noted of her comedy, 'it isn't difficult to assume great shyness behind this humour, some embarrassment to show her feelings'.[12] This inhibition gives rise to the element of heartlessness I have noted in her work, which is the necessary climate for laughter. Bergson makes clear that laughter cannot coexist with sympathetic feelings: 'indifference is its natural environment, for laughter has no greater foe than emotion'.[23] We do not laugh at a man slipping on a banana skin if we are simultaneously concerned that he is hurt. Muriel Spark's comic indifference, as well as being a protective carapace for her feelings, is also related to her faith. Like Evelyn Waugh, she sees an appalling abyss between the realms of God and man. Her comedy, while suggesting a superior attitude to the rest of mankind, is really a method of covering her fearful vision in which she, too, is on the wrong side of the abyss. Thus the novels are rich in comic distractions, and the sheer pleasure of Mrs Spark's wit and humour often deflects the reader from their more serious implications.

Her humour is most often at the level of style, although her work contains black comedy and also set pieces of 'situation comedy', such as the mock-epic battle between Percy Mannering and Guy Leet in *Memento Mori* and the funeral tea-party in the same novel. This stylistic humour is not only achieved by the incongruous juxtaposition of registers that I have already mentioned, but also by the exploitation of her aptitude for parody and her acute ear for dialogue. Mrs Spark is keenly aware of the nuances of language, and indeed, has written a short story ('You Should Have Seen the Mess') the point of which is wholly dependent on the language register of the first-person narrator. Jargon is a principal satiric target, and she creates characters who, in their devotion to fashionable trends, satirise themselves almost every time they open their mouths. In *The Driver's Seat* she makes fun of the macrobiotic cult: 'It should do well in Naples once we get the youth movement started. It's to be called the Yin-Yang Young' (p. 55). In *The Takeover* she mocks the trendy Jesuit priests who are studying 'ecological paganism': 'The younger priest sipped his drink and looked over the still lake in its deep crater and the thick wildwood of Nemi's fertile soil. "Terrific ecology!" he said. "You mean the view?" Pauline said' (p. 16). Father Gerard bends over backwards to accommodate divergent beliefs under the umbrella of Catholicism:

'Mary listed for me many cases of surviving nature-practices and superstitions in that area. They're devout Catholics, of course. I'm not saying anything against their faith; those peasants are great Catholics.'

'But they worship the tree-spirits and the water-spirits', said Hubert.

'No, no, I wouldn't say worship. You've got it wrong. The Church continues to absorb many pagan nature-rituals because the Church is ecology-conscious.' (p. 105)

His jargon is not restricted to religious matters. The younger priest fidgets on his chair, and Hubert asks if the chair is comfortable. His colleague excuses him earnestly:

'Cuthbert very often motionizes,' Gerard explained with well-wined pleasantness, 'while verbalizing, depending upon the emotive force of the topic in its relation to the scope and limitations inherent in the process of verbalization.'

'I see', said Hubert. . . . (pp. 103–4)

The jargon of solemn cults (including Christianity) is often funny or absurd to non-initiates, since it is the fervent belief in a cult which validates its language. In order to avoid the fault she satirises in others, Mrs Spark does not use elaborate theological terminology when her narrators speak of Christian faith, even though the register is often heightened and the prose more lyrical. As a general rule in her novels the more complex the jargon the more she arouses our suspicions as to the inanities it conceals. Thus American psychotherapists are high on the list for her satiric attention. Garven, in *The Hothouse by the East River*, calls himself a Guidance Director, and explains his technique: 'Through Annie I am getting to know you, Paul. It's the secondary associative process of the oblique approach. And through you I have a tertiary oblique approach to Elsa' (p. 154). A colleague continues,

> When we've had enough experience, primary, secondary and tertiary, then we can really start curative treatment on your wife, Paul. I have a new method. . . . my new method does not involve the personality of the subject and therefore the impetus to therapy-resistance is obliviated. My new method is strictly bio-psychological. (p. 155)

Jargon includes clichés, and as early as *The Comforters* Mrs Spark expresses her irritation at clichés and convenient labels used to avoid a more taxing process of thought which might lead to an altogether different conclusion. Someone says to Caroline of a mutual acquaintance, 'She's so awfully bourgeois' (p. 87), and the narrator is unusually explicit in denigrating this slipshod use of words, which is shown to depress Caroline because 'it was part of the dreary imprecise language of this half-world she had left behind her more than two years since' (p. 87). There is a moral implication here, that not only laziness but also dishonesty is involved if words are carelessly or deliberately misused. Worse still is the exploitation of others, less fluent, who are naïve enough to believe that if words are incomprehensible they must somehow be nearer to the truth than an idea simply expressed. The Abbess of Crewe is highly skilled in manipulating people through jargon, and instantly recognises its use by other people. In mocking Felicity's idiom, she expresses her contempt of her campaign against the convent, which Alexandra is certain will be ineffectual 'let Felicity tell it like it was as she may' (p. 25). Dougal Douglas is Mrs Spark's sharpest scrutineer of language. He is ghosting the autobiography of an elderly actress, and in his notebook he collects suitable clichés. The actress is anxious that Dougal should gloss over unpleasant facts, and he chooses clichés as totally appropriate for the story of her life. These include hilarious phrases such as

I thrilled to his touch.
In that moment of silent communion we renewed our shattered
   faith.
He was always an incurable romantic.
Autumn again. Autumn. The burning of leaves in the park.
I had no eyes for any other man.
I felt a grim satisfaction.
They were poles apart.

We may find these very funny, but, disconcertingly, Mrs Spark is
quite capable of hitting out at her readers' smugness in aligning with
the narrator's superiority. For example, in her short story 'The
Portobello Road' we are told that 'He looked as if he would murder
me and he did' (*Collected Stories I*, p. 29). The cliché is suddenly
revitalised. In Mrs Spark's novels people who look as if they would
murder usually do, and stale language is never used except on purpose.

Parody is a satiric device effected through style which Mrs Spark
enjoys, and she is particularly adept at subverting other literary
genres. Her novels include parodies of sensational newspaper
journalism, various epistolary styles (including a Shavian postcard),
poetry, popular fiction and schoolgirl fantasy. In *The Prime of Miss
Jean Brodie* we are given extracts from a tale called 'The Mountain
Eyrie'. It is written by Sandy and Jenny, and is a pastiche of Miss
Brodie's style and that of Robert Louis Stevenson:

> His black eye flashed in the lamplight of the hut. 'Back, girl!' he
> cried, 'and do not bar my way. Well do I know that yon girl Jenny
> will report my whereabouts to my mocking erstwhile fiancé. Well
> do I know that you are both spies sent by her that she might mock.
> Stand back from the door, I say!'
> 'Never!' said Sandy, placing her young lithe body squarely in
> front of the latch and her arm through the bolt. Her large eyes
> flashed with an azure light of appeal.
> Sandy handed the pencil to Jenny. 'It's your turn', she said.
> (p. 21)

The girls' writing is not a wholly satiric target since tacit approval is
given to their imaginative gifts, and they are, after all, still learning to
write. Mrs Spark is less kind to adult novelists, however. In *Territorial
Rights* she turns her attention to the type of realistic, contemporary
English novel in which unhappily married people dwell moodily and

at length on their relationships with each other and their respective lovers. The extracts are taken from Anthea Leaver's library book, 'a novel comfortingly like the last novel she had read'.

> Matt and Joyce finished their supper in semi-silence. Somehow she couldn't bring herself to ask the vital question: had he got the job? Was it so vital, was anything so vital anyway?
>
> If he had got the job he would have said so without her asking.
>
> Matt got up and stacked the dishes. She followed him into the kitchen and ran the hot tap. What had there ever been between them? Had it all been an illusion? The rain poured outside. Mamie's knickers and two of John's pullovers were drying in the kitchen. She looked at the damp clothes and found no significance in them. Matt looked at the kitchen clock. 'Half-past ten. I must have been late!' he exclaimed.
>
> 'You were late', she remarked, slipping the dishes into the drying-rack.
>
> Matt stood, unmoving.
>
> 'Colin and Beryl rang', she sighed. (p. 64)

An extract from this novel (which includes children called John, Mark, Mamie and Khorinthia) is quoted at the end of scenes showing Anthea in Birmingham, and is used each time to emphasise the boredom of her life compared with the exciting adventures the other characters are enjoying in Venice. This extract makes a further point, however. By her parody Mrs Spark is drawing a distinction between its tone and that of her own work, and she conveys the difference through the use of a variety of techniques she normally omits. These include an interior point of view, rhetorical questions, clichés, redundant adjectives, and euphemistic evasions of 'said'. The greatest difference, however, is the self-conscious dwelling on some kind of quest for 'significance'. This is in total contrast to the brisk, no-nonsense tone of a typical Sparkian novel with its Catholic emphasis on deeds, not motives. Mrs Spark insinuates from the dreary tone of her parodies that the novelist should not attempt too much in the way of emphasising 'significance' or 'meaning', but rather rely on presenting words and deeds to evoke the reader's own evaluation of them. She is not an anxious author, forever nudging the reader towards the right conclusion. If it is not arrived at, one feels that she would be neither despondent nor surprised. 'Readers', she has said, 'are a very meagre species.'[24]

It is difficult to draw firm conclusions about the work of a living writer, particularly one like Muriel Spark whose literary development has been unpredictable. *The Mandelbaum Gate* and *The Takeover* were unexpected departures from the short, succinct works preceding them, and *Loitering with Intent* showed a combination of warmth and wit unprecedented in her work. There is always the possibility of surprise on reading a new Muriel Spark novel; her versatile reaction to worldly trends is one of her great strengths. To summarise, what has remained consistent for over quarter of a century is the felicity of her style which is characterised by confidence and reticence: confidence in the validity of her poetic vision, reticence in her expression of it. Her style conveys more than the words actually say, since her refusal to engage openly in profundities directs our attention away from the surface realism to its inherent metaphor. And at the heart of Mrs Spark's work is her belief in God, which dictates the angle of her vision. She sees this contingent world within the control of God's purposeful plot, and the economy of this viewpoint pervades her writing. In her early novels she examines the effects of conversion and the problem of living as a Roman Catholic. Her middle novellas focus on a world where form is elevated to a God-like status, where appearances and patterning are increasingly a substitute for faith, and where emotion in such a context becomes 'indecent exposure'. Later novels contain characters ever more anarchic, whose adaptation to a godless world is portrayed satirically, yet not without a certain authorial admiration of their capacity for survival. Mrs Spark does not communicate depression at the anarchy she describes, since for her it is not the only reality. Her novels are still written *sub specie aeternitatis*, and their hallmark is a refusal to take too seriously the trappings of this world, however much they are relished and described.

Throughout Mrs Spark's work there is a tension between God's eternal status and man's temporal allegiances. As I have suggested in the course of this book, there is also another tension in her work. This is between her recognition of the formal demands of her art and the mute claims of her characters for narratorial recognition of their humanity, that is to say, for love. This is not a dominant claim in contemporary fiction, nor is it a fashionable concern of critics. Nevertheless, wherever characters are created, it persists. In Mrs Spark's novels her affection is for her most outrageous characters (Suzi and Abdul Ramdez, the Abbess of Crewe, Maggie Radcliffe, Edwina Oliver), almost as if their very outrageousness and obvious ability to survive protect her from the charge of sentimentality. But there are other, less extravagant characters such as Lise, Daphne du Toit, Charmian Colston, Ronald Bridges, Annabel Christopher, whose predicaments are described sparely, and for whom no open affection is shown. But they command our feelings none the less, because at some point in the narrative their lives are granted dignity: Charmian's perilous and courageous fight to maintain her independence, Ronald coping with his disabling illness, Annabel's refusal to be blackmailed, the posthumous narratorial restitution of Daphne and Lise.

Muriel Spark's fiction is primarily concerned with the relationship between God and man, and with the relationship of the novelist with the novel. But, paradoxically, her finest writing is achieved when the elegance of her prose is disturbed to admit the humanity of her characters and, in addition to revealing them as part of a divine pattern, she pays perceptive attention to their evident mortality.

Notes

NOTES TO CHAPTER ONE: THE SPARKIAN DISTINCTION

1. Muriel Spark, 'How I Became a Novelist', *John O'London's Weekly*, III, no. 61 (1 Dec 1960) p. 683.
2. See James Gindin, *Postwar British Fiction: New Accents and Attitudes* (London: Cambridge University Press, 1962); Rubin Rabinovitz, *The Reaction against Experiment in the English Novel 1950–1960* (New York and London: Columbia University Press, 1967); and Frederick R. Karl, *A Reader's Guide to the Contemporary English Novel* (London: Thames & Hudson, 1963), esp. ch. XII.
3. Patricia Hodgart, 'No Angry Young Women?', *Manchester Guardian Weekly*, 28 Feb 1957, p. 10.
4. All quotations from Muriel Spark's novels are taken from the editions published by Macmillan, London, except those from *Loitering with Intent*, which is published by The Bodley Head, London.
5. Graham Greene, 'Frederick Rolfe: Edwardian Inferno', in *Collected Essays* (Harmondsworth, Middx: Penguin, 1970) p. 132.
6. John Donne, 'An Anatomie of the World: the First Anniversary'.
7. Saul Bellow, 'Some Notes on Recent American Fiction', in *The Novel Today: Contemporary Writers on Modern Fiction*, ed. Malcolm Bradbury (London: Fontana, 1977) p. 56.
8. Alain Robbe-Grillet, quoted by Stephen Heath in *The Nouveau Roman: A Study in the Practice of Writing* (London: Paul Elek, 1972) p. 31.
9. Jonathan Raban, 'Criction', *London Magazine*, X, no. 2 (May 1970) pp. 89–94.
10. Roland Barthes, 'Criticism as Language', in *Twentieth-Century Literary Criticism*, ed. David Lodge (London: Longman, 1972) p. 650.
11. Muriel Spark, interview with Philip Toynbee, *Observer Colour Supplement*, 7 Nov 1971, p. 73.
12. Muriel Spark, interview with Ian Gillham, BBC World Service programme, *Writers of Today*. Abridged as 'Keeping It Short', *Listener*, 24 Sep 1970, p. 411. All my quotations are taken from the unabridged transcript.
13. Warner Berthoff, 'Fortunes of the Novel: Muriel Spark and Iris Murdoch', *Massachusetts Review*, VIII, no. 2 (Spring 1967) p. 313.
14. Douglas Reed, 'Taking Cocktails with Life', *Books and Bookmen*, XVII (11 Aug 1971) p. 14.
15. John Updike, 'Creatures of the Air', *New Yorker*, 30 Sep 1961, p. 161.
16. Frank Kermode, 'Muriel Spark', *Modern Essays* (London: Fontana, 1971) p. 267.
17. Frank Kermode, *The Sense of an Ending: Studies in the Theory of Fiction* (New York: Oxford University Press, 1967; paperback 1968) p. 131.

18. Spark–Gillham interview, transcript.
19. Muriel Spark, 'The Desegregation of Art', The Blashfield Foundation Address, *Proceedings of the American Academy of Arts and Letters 1971*, p. 24.
20. Ibid., p. 25.
21. Henry James, Preface to 'The Lesson of the Master', *The Art of the Novel: Critical Prefaces* (New York: Charles Scribner's Sons, 1962) p. 222.

NOTES TO CHAPTER TWO: BACKGROUND
1. Muriel Spark, 'The Brontës as Teachers', *New Yorker*, 22 Jan 1966, p. 33.
2. Muriel Spark, 'My Conversion', *Twentieth Century*, CLXX (Autumn 1961) p. 58.
3. Spark–Toynbee interview, *Observer Colour Supplement*, 7 Nov 1971.
4. Muriel Spark, interview with Malcolm Muggeridge, unpublished transcript of Granada Television interview *Appointment with . . .* (transmitted 2 June 1961). I am grateful to Peter Kemp for giving me a copy of this transcript.
5. Spark–Gillham interview, transcript.
6. Muriel Spark, 'What Images Return', in *Memoirs of a Modern Scotland*, ed. Karl Miller (London: Faber & Faber, 1970) p. 152. First published as 'Edinburgh-born', *New Statesman*, 10 Aug 1962, p. 180.
7. Muriel Spark, unpublished letter to Derek Stanford, 27 Feb 1952, in Muriel Spark Collection, Washington University Libraries, St Louis, Missouri.
8. Muriel Spark, interview with Alex Hamilton, *Guardian*, 8 Nov 1974, p. 10.
9. Spark–Gillham interview, transcript.
10. Muriel Spark, interview with Graham Lord, 'The Love Letters that Muriel Spark Refused to Buy', *Sunday Express*, 4 Mar 1973, p 6.
11. Muriel Spark, unpublished letter to Derek Stanford, 20 Apr 1949, in Muriel Spark Collection, Washington University Libraries.
12. Muriel Spark, *Child of Light: A Reassessment of Mary Wollstonecraft Shelley* (Hadleigh, Essex: Tower Bridge Publications, 1951) p. 3.
13. Spark, in *Memoirs of a Modern Scotland*, pp. 152–3.
14. Spark, *Child of Light*, p. 193.
15. Muriel Spark, *John Masefield* (London: Macmillan, 1962) p. 184. (First published London: Peter Nevill, 1953.)
16. Spark–Toynbee interview, *Observer Colour Supplement*, 7 Nov 1971, p. 73.
17. Spark–Muggeridge interview, transcript.
18. Spark, in *Twentieth Century*, CLXX (Autumn 1961) p. 59.
19. Muriel Spark, interview with Mary Holland, 'The Prime of Muriel Spark', *Observer Colour Supplement*, 17 Oct 1965, p. 8.
20. Muriel Spark, editorial in *Poetry Review*, XXXIX, no. 3 (Aug–Sep 1948) p. 235.
21. Spark–Muggeridge interview, transcript.
22. Ibid.
23. Spark, in *Twentieth Century*, CLXX (Autumn 1961) pp. 60, 61.
24. Frederick Karl, *A Reader's Guide to the Contemporary English Novel* (London: Thames & Hudson, 1963) p. 280.
25. Frank Kermode, 'Sheerer Spark', *Listener*, 24 Sep 1970, pp. 425–6.
26. Spark–Gillham interview, transcript.
27. See Carol B. Ohmann's analysis of *Robinson* as a Freudian allegory: 'Muriel Spark's *Robinson*', *Critique: Studies in Modern Fiction*, VIII (Fall 1965) pp. 70–84.
28. Spark–Holland interview, *Observer Colour Supplement*, 17 Oct 1965, p. 10.

29. Derek Stanford, *Inside the Forties: Literary Memoirs 1937–1957* (London: Sidgwick & Jackson, 1977) p. 205.
30. Muriel Spark, unpublished letter to John Smith, 28 Oct 1962, in Muriel Spark Collection, Washington University Libraries.
31. Muriel Spark, unpublished letter to John Smith, 25 Apr 1961, ibid.
32. Muriel Spark, in *Memoirs of a Modern Scotland*, p. 151.
33. Spark–Gillham interview, transcript.
34. Muriel Spark, unpublished letter to John Smith, 3 July 1961, Muriel Spark Collection, Washington University Libraries.
35. Spark–Toynbee interview, *Observer Colour Supplement*, 7 Nov 1971, p. 73.
36. Muriel Spark, interview with Elizabeth Jane Howard, 'Writers in the Present Tense', *Queen*, Aug 1961, p. 143.
37. Spark–Holland interview, *Observer Colour Supplement*, 17 Oct 1965, p. 10.
38. Muriel Spark, interview with George Armstrong, *Guardian*, 30 Sep 1970, p. 8.
39. Muriel Spark, unpublished letter to John Smith, n.d. (*c.* Sep 1961), in Muriel Spark Collection, Washington University Libraries.
40. Muriel Spark, unpublished letter to John Smith, 15 Aug 1961, ibid.
41. Spark–Holland interview, *Observer Colour Supplement*, 17 Oct 1965, and Spark–Gillham interview, transcript.

NOTES TO CHAPTER THREE: RELIGIOUS FAITH

1. George Orwell, *Inside the Whale and Other Essays* (Harmondsworth, Middx: Penguin, 1975) p. 39. (First published 1957.)
2. Jacques Maritain, *Art and Scholasticism*, trs. J. F. Scanlan (London: Sheed & Ward, 1923; repr. 1930) pp. 225–6.
3. Ibid., p. 70.
4. J. H. Newman, *The Idea of a University* (New York: Image Books, 1959) p. 285. (First published 1852.)
5. Maritain, *Art and Scholasticism*, pp. 224–5.
6. Graham Greene, *Ways of Escape* (London: The Bodley Head, 1980) p. 120.
7. Evelyn Waugh, *The Diaries of Evelyn Waugh*, ed. Michael Davie (London: Weidenfeld & Nicolson, 1976) pp. 778–9.
8. Ibid., p. 779.
9. John Bayley, *The Characters of Love: A Study in the Literature of Personality* (London: Chatto & Windus, 1960; paperback 1968) pp. 7–8.
10. Christopher Ricks, 'Extreme Instances', *New York Review of Books*, 19 Dec 1968, pp. 31–2.
11. Waugh, *Diaries*, p. 787.
12. Muriel Spark, interview with Frank Kermode, 'The House of Fiction', *Partisan Review*, XXX, no. 1 (Spring 1963) p. 81; repr. in *The Novel Today*, pp. 111–35.
13. William James, *The Varieties of Religious Experience: Being the Gifford Lectures on Natural Religion delivered at Edinburgh 1901–1902* (New York: Image Books, 1978) pp. 202–3. (First published 1902.)
14. Spark–Muggeridge interview, transcript.
15. Spark-Gillham interview, transcript.
16. Ibid.
17. J. H. Newman, *Apologia Pro Vita Sua* (Glasgow: Collins, Fount, 1977) p. 96. (First published 1864.)

18. Geoffrey Faber, *Oxford Apostles: A Character Study of the Oxford Movement* (London: Faber & Faber, 1933; paperback, Penguin, 1954) p. 35.
19. Ibid., p. 36.
20. Spark, in *Twentieth Century*, CLXX (Autumn 1961) p. 59.
21. Ibid.
22. Donat O'Donnell, *Maria Cross: Imaginative Patterns in a Group of Modern Catholic Writers* (London: Chatto & Windus, 1953) p. 24.
23. Derek Stanford, 'The Work of Muriel Spark: an Essay on her Fictional Method', *Month*, XXVIII (Aug 1962) p. 95.
24. Muriel Spark, 'The Religion of an Agnostic: a Sacramental View of the World in the Writings of Proust', *Church of England Newspaper*, 27 Nov 1953, p. 1.
25. Ibid.
26. Spark, in *Twentieth Century*, CLXX (Autumn 1961) p. 61.
27. Muriel Spark interview with Joyce Emerson, 'The Mental Squint of Muriel Spark', *The Sunday Times*, 30 Sep 1962, p. 14.
28. Peter Kemp, *Muriel Spark* (London: Paul Elek, 1974) p. 40.
29. Spark, 'The Religion of an Agnostic', *Church of England Newspaper*, 27 Nov 1953.
30. Ibid.
31. Muriel Spark, 'The Portobello Road', *Collected Stories I*, p. 30.

NOTES TO CHAPTER FOUR: SECULAR INFLUENCES

1. Gerard Manley Hopkins, 'The Wreck of the Deutschland', stanza 10.
2. Henry James, Preface to 'The Tragic Muse', in *The Art of the Novel: Critical Prefaces* (New York: Charles Scribner's Sons, 1962) p. 84.
3. Angus Wilson, 'Journey to Jerusalem', *Observer*, 17 Oct 1965, p. 28.
4. Spark–Holland interview, *Observer Colour Supplement*, 17 Oct 1965, p. 10.
5. Spark–Gillham interview, transcript.
6. A novelist concerned with the effect of these reforms is David Lodge. See *The British Museum is Falling Down* (London: MacGibbon & Kee, 1965); and *How Far Can You Go?* (London: Secker & Warburg, 1980).
7. Evelyn Waugh, quoted by Christopher Sykes in *Evelyn Waugh: A Biography* (Harmondsworth, Middx: Penguin, 1977) p. 596. (First published London: Collins, 1975.)
8. Spark–Hamilton interview, *Guardian*, 8 Nov 1974.
9. Spark–Armstrong interview, *Guardian*, 30 Sep 1970.
10. Spark, in *Proceedings of the American Academy of Arts and Letters 1971*, p. 26.
11. Muriel Spark, 'Bang-bang You're Dead', *Collected Stories I*, p. 87.
12. Søren Kierkegaard, *Fear and Trembling*, trs. Walter Lowrie (Princeton, N.J.: Princeton University Press, 1941; repr. 1952) pp. 66–7.
13. François Mauriac, quoted by Robert Speaight in *François Mauriac: A Study of the Writer and the Man* (London: Chatto & Windus, 1976) pp. 193–4.

NOTES TO CHAPTER FIVE: PLOTS AND PLOTTERS

1. Graham Greene, *The End of the Affair* (Harmondsworth, Middx: Penguin, 1968) pp. 181–2. (First published 1951.)

2. Angus Wilson, *The Wild Garden, or Speaking of Writing* (London: Secker & Warburg, 1963) p. 146.
3. Spark–Gillham interview, transcript.
4. John Updike, 'Topnotch Witcheries', *New Yorker*, 6 Jan 1975, p. 76.
5. David Lodge, 'The Uses and Abuses of Omniscience: Method and Meaning in Muriel Spark's *The Prime of Miss Jean Brodie*', *The Novelist at the Crossroads and Other Essays on Fiction and Criticism* (London: Routledge & Kegan Paul, 1971) pp. 119–44.
6. Ibid.
7. Graham Greene, interview with Christopher Burstall, 'Graham Greene Takes the Orient Express', *Listener*, 21 Nov 1968, p. 676.
8. Graham Greene in a letter written to V. S. Pritchett, 1948. Quoted by V. S. Pritchett in 'Graham Greene into the Light', *The Times*, 18 Mar 1978, p. 6.
9. Spark–Hamilton interview, *Guardian*, 8 Nov 1974.
10. Muriel Spark interview with Lorna Sage, 'The Prime of Muriel Spark', *Observer*, 30 May 1976, p. 11.
11. It should be noted that there is a misprint in this final paragraph of *The Public Image* in the first Penguin edition (1970) p. 125. The words 'to rest on her hip, conscious also of the baby' have been omitted. The first edition of the novel (London: Macmillan, 1968) and the Penguin reprint (Harmondsworth, Middx: Penguin, 1975) are correct.
12. Malcolm Bradbury, 'Muriel Spark's Fingernails', *Possibilities: Essays on the State of the Novel* (London: Oxford University Press, 1973) p. 253.
13. Ibid., p. 247.
14. James, Preface to 'The Lesson of the Master', *The Art of the Novel*.
15. Spark–Muggeridge interview, transcript.

NOTES TO CHAPTER SIX: STRUCTURE AND STYLE
1. Spark, in *John O'London's Weekly*, III, no. 61, p. 683.
2. Spark–Emerson interview, *The Sunday Times*, 30 Sep 1962.
3. J. H. Newman, *Letters*, ed. Derek Stanford and Muriel Spark (London: Peter Owen, 1957) p. 147.
4. Spark–Muggeridge interview, transcript.
5. Ibid.
6. Spark–Kermode interview, in *The Novel Today*, p. 133.
7. Spark, *John Masefield*, p. 67.
8. Spark–Muggeridge interview, transcript.
9. See Iris Murdoch's essay 'Against Dryness', in *The Novel Today*, pp. 22–31.
10. Spark, in *Twentieth Century*, CLXX (Autumn 1961) p. 63.
11. 'Meal for a Masochist', *The Times Literary Supplement*, 25 Sep 1970, p. 1074.
12. Mircea Eliade, *Myths, Dreams and Mysteries: The Encounter between Contemporary Faiths and Archaic Reality*, trs. Philip Mairet (Glasgow: Collins, Fontana, 1968) p. 30. (First published 1960.)
13. Spark–Kermode interview, in *The Novel Today*.
14. Spark, in *Church of England Newspaper*, 27 Nov 1953.
15. Spark, in *Twentieth Century*, CLXX (Autumn 1961) p. 62.
16. Spark–Kermode interview, in *The Novel Today*.

17. Spark–Muggeridge interview, transcript.
18. Jonathan Raban, 'A Stranger in the World', *New Review*, III, no. 31 (Oct 1976) p. 57.
19. Spark–Howard interview, in *Queen*, Aug 1961, p. 137.
20. Edmund Wilson, 'An Analysis of Max Beerbohm', *New Yorker*, 1 May 1948, p. 83.
21. Spark, in *Memoirs of a Modern Scotland*, p. 153.
22. Henk Meijer Romijn, 'Het Satirische Talent van Muriel Spark', *Tirade*, VI (1962) p. 162. I am grateful to Tony de Vletter for providing a translation of this article.
23. Henri Bergson, 'Laughter', in *Comedy*, ed. Wylie Sypher (New York: Doubleday Anchor Books, 1956) p. 63.
24. Spark–Gillham interview, transcript.

Bibliography

WORKS BY MURIEL SPARK

(a) *Fiction and Verse*

The Fanfarlo and Other Verse (Aldington, Kent: The Hand and Flower Press, 1952).
The Comforters (London: Macmillan, 1957; paperback, Penguin, 1963; Philadelphia, Penn.: J. B. Lippincott, 1957; US paperback, Avon, 1964).
The Go-Away Bird and Other Stories (London: Macmillan, 1958; paperback, Penguin, 1963; Philadelphia, Penn.: J. B. Lippincott, 1960; US paperback, Lippincott Keystone, 1961).
Robinson (London: Macmillan, 1958; paperback, Penguin, 1964; Philadelphia, Penn.: J. B. Lippincott, 1958; US paperback, Avon, 1964).
Memento Mori (London: Macmillan, 1959; paperback, Penguin, 1961; Philadelphia, Penn.: J. B. Lippincott, 1959; US paperbacks, Meridian Books, 1960, and Avon, 1966).
The Ballad of Peckham Rye (London: Macmillan, 1960; paperback, Penguin, 1963; Philadelphia, Penn.: J. B. Lippincott, 1960; US paperback, Dell, 1964).
The Bachelors (London: Macmillan, 1960; paperback, Penguin, 1963; Philadelphia, Penn.: J. B. Lippincott, 1961; US paperback, Dell, 1964).
Voices at Play: Stories and Ear-pieces (London: Macmillan, 1961; Philadelphia, Penn.: J. B. Lippincott, 1962).
The Prime of Miss Jean Brodie (first published in the *New Yorker*, 1961; London: Macmillan, 1961; paperback, Penguin, 1965; Philadelphia, Penn.: J. B. Lippincott, 1962; US paperback, Dell, 1964).
Doctors of Philosophy (London: Macmillan, 1963; New York: Alfred A. Knopf, 1966).
The Girls of Slender Means (London: Macmillan, 1963; paperback, Penguin, 1966; New York: Alfred A. Knopf, 1963; US paperback, Avon, 1964).
The Mandelbaum Gate (London: Macmillan, 1965; paperback, Penguin, 1967; New York: Alfred A. Knopf, 1965; US paperback, Fawcett, 1967).
Collected Poems I (London: Macmillan, 1967; New York: Alfred A. Knopf, 1968).
Collected Stories I (London: Macmillan, 1967; New York: Alfred A. Knopf, 1968).
The Public Image (London: Macmillan, 1968; paperback, Penguin, 1970; New York: Alfred A. Knopf, 1968; US paperback, Ballantine, 1969).
The Very Fine Clock (London: Macmillan, 1969; New York: Alfred A. Knopf, 1968).

The Driver's Seat (London: Macmillan, 1970; paperback, Penguin, 1974; New York: Alfred A. Knopf, 1970; US paperback, Bantam, 1975).

Not to Disturb (London: Macmillan, 1971; paperback, Penguin, 1974; New York: Viking Press, 1972; US paperback, Penguin, 1977).

The Hothouse by the East River (London: Macmillan, 1973; paperback, Penguin, 1975; New York: Viking Press, 1973; US paperback, Penguin, 1977).

The Abbess of Crewe (London: Macmillan, 1974; paperback, Penguin, 1975; New York: Viking Press, 1974).

The Takeover (London: Macmillan, 1976; paperback, Penguin, 1978; New York: Viking Press, 1976; US paperback, Penguin, 1978).

Territorial Rights (London: Macmillan, 1979; paperback, Panther, 1980; New York: Coward, McCann & Geoghegan, 1979).

Loitering with Intent (London: The Bodley Head, 1981; New York: Coward, McCann & Geoghegan, 1981).

(b) *Criticism*

Tribute to Wordsworth: A Miscellany of Opinion for the Centenary of the Poet's Death, ed. with Derek Stanford (London: Wingate, 1950).

Child of Light: A Reassessment of Mary Wollstonecraft Shelley (Hadleigh, Essex: Tower Bridge Publications, 1951; reissued by London: Macmillan, 1963).

A Selection of Poems by Emily Brontë, ed. with an introduction (London: Grey Walls Press, 1952).

The Brontë Letters, ed. with an introduction (London: Peter Nevill, 1953; Norman, Okla.: University of Oklahoma Press, 1954; reissued London: Macmillan, 1966).

Emily Brontë: Her Life and Work, ed. with Derek Stanford (London: Peter Owen, 1953).

My Best Mary: Selected Letters of Mary Shelley, ed. with Derek Stanford (London: Wingate, 1953).

John Masefield (London: Peter Nevill, 1953; reissued London: Macmillan, 1962; New York: Coward & McCann, 1966).

J. H. Newman's Letters, ed. with Derek Stanford (London: Peter Owen, 1957).

(c) *Articles*

'The Religion of an Agnostic: a Sacramental View of the World in the Writings of Proust', *Church of England Newspaper*, 27 Nov 1953, p. 1.

'The Mystery of Job's Suffering', *Church of England Newspaper*, 15 Apr 1955, p. 7.

'How I Became a Novelist', *John O'London's Weekly*, III, no. 61, 1 Dec 1960, p. 683.

'My Conversion', *Twentieth Century*, CLXX (Autumn 1961) pp. 58–63.

Foreword to *Realizations: Newman's Selection of his Parochial and Plain Sermons*, introduction by V. F. Blehl, SJ (London: Darton, Longman & Todd, 1964).

'The Poet's House', *Encounter*, XXX, no. 5 (5 May 1968) pp. 48–50.

'What Images Return', in *Memoirs of a Modern Scotland*, ed. Karl Miller (London: Faber & Faber, 1970) pp. 151–3.

'The Desegregation of Art', The Blashfield Foundation Address, *Proceedings of the American Academy of Arts and Letters 1971*, pp. 21–7.

(d) *Interviews*

Interview with Malcolm Muggeridge, *Appointment with* ..., Granada Television, transmitted 2 June 1961. Unpublished transcript.

Interview with Elizabeth Jane Howard, 'Writers in the Present Tense', *Queen*, Aug 1961, pp. 136–46.

Interview with Joyce Emerson, 'The Mental Squint of Muriel Spark', *The Sunday Times*, 30 Sep 1962, p. 14.

Interview with Frank Kermode, 'The House of Fiction: Interviews with Seven English Novelists', *Partisan Review*, XXX, no. 1 (Spring 1963) pp. 61–82; repr. in *The Novel Today: Contemporary Writers on Modern Fiction*, ed. Malcolm Bradbury (London: Collins, Fontana, 1977) pp. 111–35.

Interview with Mary Holland, 'The Prime of Muriel Spark', *Observer Colour Supplement*, 17 Oct 1965, pp. 8–10.

Interview with George Armstrong, *Guardian*, 30 Sep 1970, p. 8.

Interview with Ian Gillham, *Writers of Today*, no. 4, BBC World Service script. Abridged as 'Keeping It Short', *Listener*, 24 Sep 1970, pp. 411–13.

Interview with Philip Toynbee, *Observer Colour Supplement*, 7 Nov 1971, p. 73.

Interview with Graham Lord, 'The Love Letters that Muriel Spark Refused to Buy', *Sunday Express*, 4 Mar 1973, p. 6.

Interview on *Kaleidoscope*, BBC Radio 4; abridged as 'Bugs and Mybug', *Listener*, 28 Nov 1974, p. 706.

Interview with Alex Hamilton, *Guardian*, 8 Nov 1974, p. 10.

Interview with Lorna Sage, 'The Prime of Muriel Spark', *Observer*, 30 May 1976, p. 11.

(e) *Letters*

Muriel Spark Collection, Washington University Libraries, St Louis, Missouri.

WORKS BY OTHER WRITERS

(a) *Additional Primary Sources*

Cellini, Benvenuto, *Life*, trs. Anne Macdonell (London: Everyman's Library, 1907).

Greene, Graham, *The End of the Affair* (Harmondsworth, Middx: Penguin, 1968). (First published 1951.)

——, *A Burnt-Out Case* (Harmondsworth, Middx: Penguin, 1963). (First published 1960.)

Kierkegaard, Søren, *Fear and Trembling*, trs. Walter Lowrie (Princeton, N.J.: Princeton University Press, 1941; repr. 1952).

Lodge, David, *The British Museum is Falling Down* (London: MacGibbon & Kee, 1965).

——, *How Far Can You Go?* (London: Secker & Warburg, 1980).

Newman, John, *Loss and Gain: The Story of a Convert* (London: Burns & Oates, Universe Books, 1962). (First published 1848.)

——, *The Idea of a University* (New York: Image Books, 1959). (First published 1852.)

——, *Apologia pro Vita Sua* (Glasgow: Collins, Fount, 1977). (First published 1864.)

Proust, Marcel, *Remembrance of Things Past*, trs. C. K. Scott Moncrieff (London: Chatto & Windus, 1966). (First published in English 1922.)
Waugh, Evelyn, *The Diaries of Evelyn Waugh*, ed. Michael Davie (London: Weidenfeld & Nicolson, 1976).

(b) *Secondary Sources: Books*

Bayley, John, *The Characters of Love: A Study in the Literature of Personality* (London: Chatto & Windus, 1960; paperback 1968).
Bergonzi, Bernard, *The Situation of the Novel* (London: Macmillan, 1970).
Bradbury, Malcolm, *Possibilities: Essays on the State of the Novel* (London: Oxford University Press, 1973).
—— (ed.), *The Novel Today: Contemporary Writers on Modern Fiction* (London: Fontana, 1977).
Burgess, Anthony, *The Novel Now* (London: Faber & Faber, 1967).
Cox, C. B., *The Free Spirit: A Study of Liberal Humanism in the Novels of George Eliot, Henry James, E. M. Forster, Virginia Woolf, Angus Wilson* (London: Oxford University Press, 1963).
Devitis, A. A., *Roman Holiday: The Catholic Novels of Evelyn Waugh* (London: Vision Press, 1958).
Eliade, Mircea, *Myths, Dreams and Mysteries: The Encounter between Contemporary Faiths and Archaic Reality*, trs. by Philip Mairet (Glasgow: Collins, Fontana, Library of Theology and Philosophy, 1968). (First published 1960.)
Faber, Geoffrey, *Oxford Apostles: A Character Study of the Oxford Movement* (London: Faber & Faber, 1933; paperback, Penguin, 1954).
Frazer, James, *The Golden Bough: A Study in Magic and Religion*, pt VII: 'Balder the Beautiful', 2 vols (London: Macmillan, 1913). (First published 1890.)
Gindin, James, *Postwar British Fiction: New Accents and Attitudes* (London: Cambridge University Press, 1962).
Goffman, Erving, *The Presentation of Self in Everyday Life* (London: Allen Lane, 1969). (First published 1959.)
Greene, Graham, *Collected Essays* (Harmondsworth, Middx: Penguin, 1970). (First published 1969.)
Harvey, W. J., *Character and the Novel* (London: Chatto & Windus, 1965).
Heath, Stephen, *The Nouveau Roman: A Study in the Practice of Writing*, in the series 'Novelists and their World' (London: Paul Elek, 1972).
James, Henry, *The Art of the Novel: Critical Prefaces* (New York: Charles Scribner's Sons, 1962).
James, William, *The Varieties of Religious Experience: Being the Gifford Lectures on Natural Religion Delivered at Edinburgh 1901–1902* (New York: Image Books, 1978).
Josipovici, Gabriel, *The World and the Book: A Study of Modern Fiction* (London: Macmillan, 1971).
—— (ed.), *The Modern English Novel: The Reader, the Writer and the Work* (London: Open Books, 1976).
Karl, Frederick R., *A Reader's Guide to the Contemporary English Novel* (London: Thames & Hudson, 1963).
Kemp, Peter, *Muriel Spark*, in the series 'Novelists and their World' (London: Paul Elek, 1974).

Kennedy, Alan, *The Protean Self: Dramatic Action in Contemporary Fiction* (London: Macmillan, 1974).

Kermode, Frank, *The Sense of an Ending: Studies in the Theory of Fiction* (New York: Oxford University Press, 1967; paperback 1968).

——, *Modern Essays* (London: Fontana, 1971).

Kinkead-Weekes, Mark, and Gregor, Ian, *William Golding: A Critical Study* (London: Faber & Faber, 1967).

Lodge, David, *The Novelist at the Crossroads and Other Essays on Fiction and Criticism* (London: Routledge & Kegan Paul, 1971).

——, *The Modes of Modern Writing: Metaphor, Metonymy and the Typology of Modern Literature* (London: Edward Arnold, 1977).

——(ed.), *Twentieth-Century Literary Criticism: A Reader* (London: Longman, 1972).

Malkoff, Karl, *Muriel Spark*, Columbia Essays on Modern Writers, no. 36 (New York and London: Columbia University Press, 1968).

Maritain, Jacques, *Art and Scholasticism*, trs. J. F. Scanlan (London: Sheed & Ward, 1923; repr. 1930).

Massie, Alan, *Muriel Spark* (Edinburgh: Ramsey Head Press, 1979).

Miller, Karl, *Memoirs of a Modern Scotland* (London: Faber & Faber, 1970).

O'Donnell, Donat, *Maria Cross: Imaginative Patterns in a Group of Modern Catholic Writers* (London: Chatto & Windus, 1953).

Orwell, George, *Inside the Whale and Other Essays* (Harmondsworth, Middx: Penguin, 1975). (First published 1957.)

Rabinovitz, Rubin, *The Reaction against Experiment in the English Novel 1950–1960* (New York and London: Columbia University Press, 1967).

Smith, George, *The Teaching of the Catholic Church*, 2 vols (London: Burns, Oates & Washbourne, 1948).

Speaight, Robert, *François Mauriac: A Study of the Writer and the Man* (London: Chatto & Windus, 1976).

Stanford, Derek, *Muriel Spark: A Biographical and Critical Study* (London: Centaur Press, 1963).

——, *Inside the Forties: Literary Memoirs 1937–1957* (London: Sidgwick & Jackson, 1977).

Stratford, Philip, *Faith and Fiction: Creative Process in Greene and Mauriac* (Notre Dame, Ind.: University of Notre Dame Press, 1964; paperback 1967).

Stubbs, Patricia, *Muriel Spark*, in the series 'Writers and their Work', no. 229, ed. Ian Scott-Kilvert (Harlow, Essex: Longman for the British Council, 1973).

Swinden, Patrick, *Unofficial Selves: Character in the Novel from Dickens to the Present Day* (London: Macmillan, 1973).

Sykes, Christopher, *Evelyn Waugh: A Biography* (Harmondsworth, Middx: Penguin, 1977). (First published 1975.)

Wilson, Angus, *The Wild Garden, or Speaking of Writing* (London: Secker & Warburg, 1963).

(c) *Selected Articles and Reviews*

Adler, Renata, 'Muriel Spark', in *On Contemporary Literature*, ed. Richard Kostelanetz (New York: Avon Books, 1964).

Baldanza, Frank, 'Muriel Spark and the Occult', *Wisconsin Studies in Contemporary Literature*, VI, no. 2 (Summer 1965) pp. 190–203.

Balliett, Whitney, 'The Burning Bush', *New Yorker*, 13 June 1959, p. 119.
Bergonzi, Bernard, 'Graham Greene Supplied the Lyrics: a Footnote to the Thirties', *Encounter*, XLVII, no. 6 (Dec 1976) pp. 67–71.
——, 'A Conspicuous Absentee: the Decline and Fall of the Catholic Novel', *Encounter*, LV, nos 2–3 (Aug–Sep 1980) pp. 44–56.
Bergson, Henri, 'Laughter', in *Comedy*, ed. Wylie Sypher (New York: Doubleday Anchor Books, 1956) pp. 61–190.
Berthoff, Warner, 'Fortunes of the Novel: Muriel Spark and Iris Murdoch', *Massachusetts Review*, VIII, no. 2 (Spring 1967) pp. 301–32.
Bradbury, Malcolm, 'Pilgrim's Progress', *New York Times Book Review*, 31 Oct 1965, pp. 4, 52.
——, 'Dark Spark', *New Society*, 24 Sep 1970, p. 555.
——, 'Muriel Spark's Fingernails', *Possibilities: Essays on the State of the Novel* (London: Oxford University Press, 1973) pp. 247–55.
Byatt, A. S., 'Whittled and Spiky Art', *New Statesman*, 15 Dec 1967, p. 848.
——, 'Empty Shell', *New Statesman*, 14 June 1968, pp. 807–8.
——, 'A Murder in Hell', *The Times*, 24 Sep 1970, p. 14.
Dobie, Ann B., '*The Prime of Miss Jean Brodie*: Muriel Spark Bridges the Credibility Gap', *Arizona Quarterly*, XXV (Autumn 1969) pp. 217–28.
——, 'Muriel Spark's Definition of Reality', *Critique*, XII, no. 1 (1970) pp. 20–7.
——, and Wooton, Carl, 'Spark and Waugh: Similarities by Coincidence', *Midwest Quarterly*, XIII (July 1972) pp. 423–34.
Enright, D. J., 'Public Doctrine and Private Judging', *New Statesman*, 15 Oct 1965, pp. 566–7.
Fallowell, Duncan, 'Campo dei Fiori', *Spectator*, 12 June 1976, p. 23.
Fay, Bernard, 'Muriel Spark en sa Fleur', *Nouvelle Revue Française*, XIV (Feb 1966) pp. 307–15.
Gilliat, Penelope, 'Black Laughs', *Spectator*, 21 Oct 1960, pp. 620–1.
Graude, Luke, 'Gabriel Fielding: New Master of the Catholic Classic', *Catholic World*, CXCVII (June 1963) pp. 172–9.
Greene, George, 'A Reading of Muriel Spark', *Thought*, XLIII (Autumn 1968) pp. 393–407.
Greene, Graham, 'Graham Greene Takes the Orient Express', interview with Christopher Burstall, *Listener*, 21 Nov 1968, pp. 672–7.
——, interview with Gavin Young, *Observer*, 12 Mar 1968, p. 35.
Gross, John, 'Passionate Pilgrimage', *New York Review of Books*, 28 Oct 1965, pp. 12–15.
Grosskurth, Phyllis, 'The World of Muriel Spark: Spirits or Spooks?', *Tamarack Review*, XXXIX (1966) pp. 62–7.
Harrison, Bernard, 'Muriel Spark and Jane Austen', in *The Modern English Novel: The Reader, the Writer and the Work*, ed. Gabriel Josipovici (London: Open Books, 1976) pp. 225–51.
Hodgart, Patricia, 'No Angry Young Women?', *Manchester Guardian Weekly*, 28 Feb 1957, p. 10.
Hoyt, Charles Alva, 'Muriel Spark: the Surrealist Jane Austen', in *Contemporary British Novelists*, ed. Charles Shapiro (Carbondale and Edwardsville: Southern Illinois University Press, 1965) pp. 125–43.
Hynes, Samuel, 'The Prime of Muriel Spark', *Commonweal*, 23 Feb 1962, pp. 562–8.
Jacobsen, Josephine, 'A Catholic Quartet: Muriel Spark, Graham Greene, J. W.

Powers, Flannery O'Connor', *Christian Scholar*, LXVII (Summer 1964) pp. 139–54.
Kermode, Frank, 'Myth, Reality and Fiction', *Listener*, 30 Aug 1962, pp. 311–13.
——, 'The Prime of Miss Muriel Spark', *New Statesman*, 27 Sep 1963, pp. 397–8.
——, 'The Novel as Jerusalem', *Atlantic Monthly*, CCXVI (Oct 1965) pp. 92–8.
——, 'Sheerer Spark', *Listener*, 24 Sep 1970, pp. 425–6.
——, 'Foreseeing the Unforeseen', *Listener*, 11 Dec 1971, pp. 657–8.
——, 'Diana of the Crossroads', *New Statesman*, 4 June 1976, pp. 746–7.
——, 'Judgement in Venice', *Listener*, 26 Apr 1979, pp. 584–5.
Lodge, David, 'Passing the Test', *Tablet*, 10 Oct 1970, p. 978.
——, 'The Uses and Abuses of Omniscience: Method and Meaning in Muriel
Spark's *The Prime of Miss Jean Brodie*', *The Novelist at the Crossroads and Other
Essays on Fiction and Criticism* (London: Routledge & Kegan Paul, 1971)
pp. 119–44.
——, 'Change from the Best', *Tablet*, 12 May 1973, pp. 442–3.
——, 'Prime Spark', *Tablet*, 7 Dec 1974, p. 1185.
——, 'Prime Cut', *New Statesman*, 27 Apr 1979, p. 597.
Malin, Irving, 'The Deceptions of Muriel Spark', in *The Vision Obscured: Perceptions
of Some Twentieth Century Novelists*, ed. Melvin J. Friedman (New York: Fordham
University Press, 1970) pp. 95–107.
Malkoff, Karl, 'Demonology and Dualism: the Supernatural in Isaac Singer and
Muriel Spark', in *Critical Views of Isaac Bashevis Singer*, ed. Irving Malin (New
York: New York University Press, 1969) pp. 149–68.
Mayne, Richard, 'Fiery Particle: on Muriel Spark', *Encounter*, XXV (6 Dec 1965)
pp. 61–8.
Miller, Karl, 'Hard Falls', *New Statesman*, 3 Nov 1961, pp. 662–3.
Murphy, Carol, 'A Spark of the Supernatural', *Approach*, LX (Summer 1966)
pp. 26–30.
Naipaul, V. S., 'Death on the Telephone', *New Statesman*, 28 Mar 1959, p. 452.
Nye, Robert, 'Another Suicide', *Guardian*, 24 Sep 1970, p. 14.
——, 'Gloria Deplores You Strikes Again', *Guardian*, 11 Nov 1971, p. 9.
Ohmann, Carol, 'Muriel Spark's *Robinson*', *Critique*, VIII (Fall 1965) pp. 70–84.
Petersen, Virgilia, 'Few Were More Delightful, Lovely or Savage', *New York Times
Book Review*, 15 Sep 1963, pp. 4, 5, 44.
Potter, Nancy, 'Muriel Spark: Transformer of the Commonplace', *Renascence*, XVII
(Spring 1965) pp. 115–20.
Price, Martin, 'In the Fielding Country: Some Recent Fiction', *Yale Review*, XLVII,
no. 1 (Autumn 1957) pp. 143–56.
——, 'The Difficulties of Commitment: Some Recent Novels', *Yale Review*, XLVIII,
no. 4 (Summer 1959) pp. 597–8.
——, 'The Self-Deceivers: Some Recent Fiction', *Yale Review*, XLVIII, no. 2 (Winter
1959) pp. 272–80.
Pritchett, V. S., 'Graham Greene into the Light', *The Times*, 18 Mar 1978, p. 6.
Raban, Jonathan, 'Criction', *London Magazine*, X, no. 2 (May 1970) pp. 89–94.
——, 'Vague Scriptures', *New Statesman*, 12 Nov 1971, pp. 657–8.
——, 'A Stranger in the World', *New Review*, III, no. 31 (Oct 1976) p. 57.
Ratcliffe, Michael, 'Hell and Chaos as Farce', *The Times*, 1 Mar 1973, p. 14.
Reed, Douglas, 'Taking Cocktails with Life', *Books and Bookmen*, XVII (11 Aug 1971)
pp. 10–14.

Ricks, Christopher, 'Extreme Instances', *New York Review of Books*, 19 Dec 1968, pp. 31–2.
Romijn, Henk Meijer, 'Het Satirische Talent van Muriel Spark', *Tirade*, VI (1962) pp. 157–69.
Sage, Lorna, 'Bugging the Nunnery', *Observer*, 10 Nov 1974, p. 33.
——, 'Roman Scandals', *Observer*, 6 June 1976, p. 29.
——, 'Vice in Venice', *Observer*, 29 Apr 1979, p. 37.
Schneider, Harold, 'A Writer in her Prime: the Fiction of Muriel Spark', *Critique*, V (Fall 1962) pp. 28–45.
Stanford, Derek, 'The Early Days of Miss Muriel Spark', *Critic*, XX, no. 5 (Apr–May 1962) pp. 49–53.
——, 'The Work of Muriel Spark: an Essay on her Fictional Method', *Month*, XXVIII (Aug 1962) pp. 92–9.
The Times Literary Supplement, 'Questing Characters', 22 Feb 1957, p. 109.
——, 'Questions and Answers', 27 June 1958, p. 357.
——, 'Sense and Sensitivity', 19 Dec 1958, p. 733.
——, 'Crabbed Age and Youth', 17 Apr 1959, p. 221.
——, 'Faith and Fancy', 4 Mar 1960, p. 141.
——, 'Stag Party', 14 Oct 1960, p. 657.
——, 'Mistress of Style', 3 Nov 1961, p. 785.
——, 'Hell in the Royal Borough', 20 Sep 1963, p. 701.
——, 'Talking about Jerusalem', 14 Oct 1965, p. 913.
——, 'Shallowness Everywhere', 13 June 1968, p. 612.
——, 'Meal for a Masochist', 25 Sep 1970, p. 1074.
——, 'Grub Street Gothic', 12 Nov 1971, p. 1409.
——, 'Shadow Boxing', 2 Mar 1973, p. 229.
Tuohy, Frank, 'Rewards and Bogies', *Spectator*, 3 Nov 1961, p. 634.
Updike, John, 'Creatures of the Air', *New Yorker*, 30 Sep 1961, pp. 161–6.
——, 'Between a Wedding and a Funeral', *New Yorker*, 14 Sep 1963, pp. 192–4.
——, 'Topnotch Witcheries', *New Yorker*, 6 Jan 1975, pp. 76–8.
Waugh, Auberon, 'New Novels', *Spectator*, 20 Nov 1971, p. 733.
——, 'Spark Plug', *Spectator*, 17 Mar 1973, pp. 331–2.
Waugh, Evelyn, 'Something Fresh', *Spectator*, 22 Feb 1957, p. 256.
——, 'Threatened Genius: Difficult Saint', *Spectator*, 7 July 1961, p. 28.
Wildman, John Hazard, 'Translated by Muriel Spark', in *Nine Essays in Modern Literature*, ed. Donald Stanford (Baton Rouge: Louisiana State University Press, 1965) pp. 129–44.
Wilson, Angus, 'Journey to Jerusalem', *Observer*, 17 Oct 1965, p. 28.
Wilson, Edmund, 'An Analysis of Max Beerbohm', *New Yorker*, 1 May 1948, p. 83.

Index